Teaching *Is* Inquiry

Teaching *Is* Inquiry

Observation and Reflection as the Heart of Practice

Cynthia Ballenger

TEACHERS COLLEGE PRESS
TEACHERS COLLEGE | COLUMBIA UNIVERSITY
NEW YORK AND LONDON

Published by Teachers College Press,® 1234 Amsterdam Avenue, New York, NY 10027

An earlier version of Chapter 5 was published as "Learning About Literature While Reading With Children," *The Educational Forum*, vol. 78, no. 4 (2014). Reprinted by permission of the publisher (Taylor & Francis Ltd, http://www.tandfonline.com).

Earlier versions of Chapters 6 and 8 were published as "Reframing the Achievement Gap: Lessons From Puzzling Students," *The Reading Teacher*, vol. 73, no. 2 (2019, Sept.–Oct.). Reprinted with permission.

An earlier version of Chapter 8 appears in C. Furman and T. de Rezenda Rocha (Eds.) (2025), *Teachers and Philosophy: Essays on the Contact Zone*, SUNY Press.

Library of Congress Cataloging-in-Publication Data is available at loc.gov

ISBN 978-0-8077-8660-4 (paper)
ISBN 978-0-8077-8661-1 (hardcover)
ISBN 978-0-8077-8283-5 (ebook)

Printed on acid-free paper
Manufactured in the United States of America

For Jack

Contents

Acknowledgments

GRATITUDE

This is not work that can be done alone.

I would like to thank my husband, above all, for reading chapters, offering suggestions, and never remaining satisfied with any easy answer, sometimes to my chagrin.

My children have read some chapters; they read as parents, as former students, as engaged citizens, and have consistently offered insightful critiques. My grandchildren, Robin, Immanuel, Cassidy, and Lilah have read some of the same books I discuss here and shared their insights with me.

Dirck Roosevelt and Susan J. Mayer have joined me in numerous conversations from which I have formed, changed, and developed my ideas. Mary Bodwell, Catherine O'Connor, Alexandra Miletta, Marty Rutherford, Sarah Michaels, Deborah Schifter, Susan Jo Russell, Cara Furman, Traci Higgins, Kathleen Boyle, and Brian Drayton, among others, have read drafts of some chapters and been enormously helpful and encouraging.

When I collapsed, unable to form a conclusion, Susan Mayer, Marty Rutherford, and Alexandra Miletta all responded to my anguished emails, reminding me that we never do this alone. Their comments and companionship were the strength I needed to finish this work.

Teaching *Is* Inquiry

Introduction

The Canary in the Coal Mine

What is teaching as inquiry? Many of us entered teaching because we found joy in watching students engage and think. This joy often diminishes as testing, institutional pressures of various sorts, and also our own daily experience of the material we teach narrows our view. I hope you will see that the process of reflection introduced here is in some ways an answer to this concern. Teaching as inquiry is not an additional task; it does not take extra time and attention. Rather, it is a way of being in the classroom that can help children and reinvigorate our own sense of the excitement of teaching and learning.

Teaching as inquiry fundamentally involves curiosity, curiosity into the ideas of all children. The central philosophical commitment of this approach is to the idea that children are always thinking and always making sense and that their ideas are relevant to serious academic and intellectual study. Always. Teaching as inquiry, or teacher research, as it is also called, is a search for all the approaches or ideas, not just the ones we're used to thinking of as correct, powerful, or on topic. Children see things we may not see; they approach ideas in many different ways. They learn from us; but also we may learn from them. Teaching as inquiry asks you to be humble, to be willing to acknowledge that you may misunderstand things, and to pay particular attention to those children who puzzle you, who seem to have ideas different from your own. Teaching as inquiry reminds us that teaching is an uncertain craft, a daily drama full of human connection, difference, occasional disappointment, surprise and also joy.

I will introduce this idea with a metaphor. This story captures the heart of what I hope to impart in the book. It represents what I have learned about students, especially those who struggle, those whose ideas and approaches I don't immediately recognize or honor.

The atmosphere in coal mines can become toxic suddenly and unexpectedly. Canaries are more sensitive to the quality of the air than the average human. Miners therefore carried canaries with them in cages into the coal mines; when the canaries began to suffer, it was a sign to the miners that there was a problem with the air in the mine, a problem which would have an effect on everyone, although the miners could not yet perceive it themselves. The canaries' responses were taken very seriously.

In this book, the canary in the classroom is the child I call the "puzzling child." The puzzling child is one many of us tend to write off as wrong or confused, one who needs more help, who struggles to explain him- or herself. The atmosphere in the coal mine represents good thinking and good behavior. When this atmosphere, when the intellectual and pedagogical assumptions that we use to construct the classroom environment, becomes stale, when it lacks fresh oxygen, these puzzling children, like the canary, let us know it first. Exploring their responses can help us to open up the mine and let in a full dose of oxygen.

Daniel was such a canary.[1] He was a 4th-grader when I knew him, the child of immigrants. His English was adequate, but his vocabulary was not large. He was seemingly unengaged in school and seldom participated in class; he did not read at grade level, nor did he like to read.

In Daniel's science class, we had placed cups of water all over the classroom: over the heaters, in cold corners near the windows, in the refrigerator, and so on. After a week, we began to check the cups of water to see how much liquid remained. I had planned to have the students make representations of the various cups and the level of water in them, and in this way I hoped to lead us eventually to draw graphs showing the different amounts of water evaporation.

As we begin, the children are noticing that the water in the hotter areas of the classroom was disappearing the fastest, something many of them had more or less expected. Daniel, in the midst of this growing consensus, asks hesitantly, "but [and he picks up one of the cups and looks intently at the bottom] it can't go out the bottom." Where has the water gone? he was asking. I ask the children to answer him, and they quickly tell him that water evaporates, that it goes up when it evaporates, not out the bottom. The discussion continues.

Daniel accepts this explanation, although, as I remember it, he does so without much enthusiasm. Many teachers, including myself, are pleased when the children help each other, and I felt that way initially. I found Daniel's question a simple one; in the moment, I believed that the children had answered it and also had taught him a new word. However, by chance I had made an audio recording of the discussion, and later, as I listened to it, I could feel his puzzled tone. I could hear that he had been thinking hard and then, as I reflected, I realized that the answer we gave him was not adequate. In fact, as I thought it over, I recognized that I didn't really know how heat causes

1. The names of all children mentioned in this volume have been changed.

water molecules to rise and leave the cup either. It is amazing when you think of it; as Daniel said later when we questioned him, "Everything else falls down." Daniel alone knew that we all were stating something that was not self-evident—he recognized that saying that "hot air rises" or that "it evaporates" was not really an explanation. He was the only one of all of us who recognized that we did not really understand this explanation. Yet had I not had the chance to listen to this conversation later, I would not have realized this. I would have felt that I had been effective in allowing the children to respond to Daniel. Daniel was the canary in the coal mine.

Who benefited from this interaction and who did not? The children who instructed Daniel had the opportunity to feel smart and competent. However, they were not aware that they did not really know the answer. They had accepted an explanation without seriously thinking it through. We don't see them exercising genuine curiosity or critical thinking. Daniel, on the other hand, asked a good question; he knew he did not understand, and that something did not make sense to him. But the response he got did not validate him nor his thinking. I, and the classroom generally, did not initially recognize his question as an important one. I had presented the subject matter of the water cycle as I had learned it, a logically consistent and endless cycle of water changing state. His question hadn't occurred to me.

Of course, teachers are all fallible. We all miss the point or the thought in what children say at times. And, more importantly, as in this case, we are also often blinded by what we think we know and thus we fail to question some of our own understanding. It is only human.

In this case, because I had made a recording of the conversation, that is, in my terms, because I had a way to "stop time" for further thinking, and because I had had the good fortune to participate in a teachers' group that encouraged me to look closely at classroom interactions of this kind, I returned to Daniel's question the next day. The students and I decided to take up Daniel's concern. We did so in a variety of ways. We made a list of "what can go up." Students who had initially felt they knew that hot air rises, now asked why, if we go high on the top of a mountain and hot air rises, it's not warmer, but colder. We thought about the temperature upstairs in our houses. We watched steam and smoke rise. Placing ice on the top of a glass jar of water, we watched condensation form and then watched the drops fall. Kids came in from recess on a cold day to tell me excitedly about watching their breath fly up, and then they wondered if it joined the clouds in the sky. Daniel's question became the basis for what was probably the most widely engaging science unit I taught that year, challenging for all students and often for me as well.

It is often children like Daniel, children perhaps less likely to have received explanations early on from their parents that they accepted and did not question, who have a better sense of what it feels like when they really understand and, in contrast, when they do not. Daniel was truly the canary who recognized the thinness of our very pat explanation, and he then helped us get beyond it. We needed Daniel.

Daniel's is a cautionary tale. It is only one of many stories I will tell in this book about instances where unquestioned expectations and conventional understandings blinded me to the power of the thinking and engagement around me. I was a science teacher and ESL teacher in Daniel's classroom. In the remaining stories in this book, I was a reading specialist and was at times in charge of the entire class, at other times, in charge of reading groups of four or five children or even individuals. In these roles I was someone who was in and out of many classrooms frequently. I will use my own teaching to illustrate these cautionary tales because I do not want to accuse anyone else of missing students' important moments or ideas, but I can assure you that the sort of thing I will describe here happens all the time in many subject areas and in the best classrooms. It is not so much a failing as an opportunity.

I will try to demonstrate in this book how the practice of finding some way to return to the event or the conversation for further reflection, to "stop time" as I did with the audio recording in this case, allows us to make reflection on children's ideas a part of the practice of teaching, and how this reflection can lead us to more democratic as well as more complete and also more joyful understanding of the range of children's thinking and ideas.

This book is separated into three parts. The first section introduces in multiple ways what teaching as research is and how to do it. The second and third are accounts of my classroom teaching: The second focuses on the experience of teaching novels in middle school, and the third is about teaching children with special needs and abilities.

Part I

At the beginning of this Introduction, I offered the story of Daniel, which contains the heart of what teaching as inquiry is. The story introduces the two crucial practices of an inquiry stance—"stopping time" and reflection—and demonstrates the value of reflecting on the ideas of "the puzzling child."

In Chapter 1, I describe the sources of this stance in the literature on education. The literature from which I learned were studies of education that were based on ethnographic accounts of real students and classrooms, that is, studies that described in detail the words and activity of the students.

The next chapter in this section is an explanation of the research practices of teaching as inquiry as I know them. What do we do, when, and why? I describe the techniques of "stopping time," ways to focus investigations, and how to find questions. Finally, I give an example from the induction of a teacher beginning to do this work.

The following two parts of the book are stories of my teaching and my students.

Part II

This section contains accounts of teaching reading.

I begin in Chapter 3 by discussing some explanations for reading failure that are commonly referenced by educators and then I introduce my own view.

Chapter 4 centers on a boy whose way of responding to our book was very different from my own and which came, I believe, from his cultural background.

Chapter 5 is an account of reading *There's a Boy in the Girls' Bathroom* by Louis Sachar with a boy who was often in trouble in school, and who did not read well or like to read. His response to this book showed me a great deal about the experience of empathy in reading stories and the uses of literature in real life.

In Chapter 6, a group of children, all immigrants, read the book *Crash* and used it to discuss their own backgrounds and to recognize similarities and differences.

Part III

This section, "Children with Special Needs," begins with an introduction to the uses of note taking with atypical children.

Chapter 7 is an account of reading with Jillian, a child who unexpectedly showed me a different view of herself when she began to talk about dinosaurs.

Chapter 8 is the story of a year assisting and observing Jessica as she brought her interest in worms into more and more areas of her social life.

In Chapter 9, the concluding chapter, I return to discuss the practices and commitments of teaching as inquiry, the strengthening, or regaining, of the joy of teaching it provides, and its place in the present-day context of education.

A Thought on How to Read This Book

Some readers may wish to start with the stories and then return to the explanatory chapters later. If that is your choice, I would recommend nevertheless to start with the introduction.

Part I

RESEARCH STANCE

CHAPTER 1

Theories and Practices

THE AIR WE BREATHE

As I said in the introduction, teaching as inquiry is inquiry into the ideas of all students. It is committed to the idea that children are always thinking and always making sense and that their ideas are relevant to serious academic and intellectual study.

In the following chapters, I hope to demonstrate the radical position that arises from this idea: that the ideas of those students we find puzzling, children like Daniel, often lead us to new recognition of, in Michael Armstrong's simple phrase, "thinking in all its forms" (Armstrong, 1990, p. 23).

Here I will describe the thinking and theories that formed this view of teaching. I begin with the idea of "culture." I write as a teacher and to teachers, and to educators more generally. Many of us, throughout our professional lives, maintain commitments to ideas and practices that we rarely question. These commitments arise from our training, our own schooling and our experience, and we generally regard them as obvious and natural. These habitual patterns of acting, of seeing, of valuing, of talking and making sense are behind many assumptions we make about how students should behave in school, how they learn, what they should learn, and what ideas we, as teachers, consider smart or thoughtful. They are the very air we breathe. And although we are hardly aware of many of these assumptions, they govern a good deal of what we do. Deborah Ball in her 2018 American Educational Research Association (AERA) presidential address coined the term "discretionary spaces" to describe those spaces where assumptions and habits come into play in the pedagogical choices teachers make; as she demonstrated, decisions are made quickly, almost automatically, and often to the detriment of some students. These areas of largely invisible cultural assumptions are what I hope to make visible.

MENTORS, COLLEAGUES, AND SCHOLARSHIP

When I began to teach it was a time of great concern about the "achievement gap," as it still is today. This term, now often replaced with "opportunity gap," in order to make clear the many elements of our social and educational context that influence school achievement (see, e.g., Ladson-Billings, 2007), brought to our attention vividly the question of whether we were reaching all our students. I joined a group of teachers to consider this question. We named ourselves the Brookline Teacher Researcher Seminar (BTRS) and I, and others, have described it in detail elsewhere (e.g., BTRS, 2004). The BTRS disbanded many years ago. In this chapter I will recount some of the learning and reading which developed as a part of this experience and became the basis for my continuing inquiries into practice.

This explanation will principally address two themes:

1. Gaining distance from unexamined assumptions about what talk in school should look like.
2. Developing a method to provide time to reflect on students' talk, ideas, and interests.

One aspect of the focus on the achievement gap was an upwelling of interest in teaching from scholars whose training had been in ethnography and linguistics. The scholars in this field were seeking to make visible the patterns of language use in school—how one talked there, when and in what forms and styles—and then, in contrast, to provide an account of the patterns and styles of language use in various communities outside school. Their focus included, in particular, those communities many of whose children were less successful in school, for example, African American children, Native Hawaiian children, Navajo children, and others. These scholars did not assume that different ways of talking and using language were not valuable, although many had made this assumption in the past. Rather, they sought to explore in their research the broad spectrum of human meaning making, in and out of school. They hoped that this broader perspective could inform educators of new ways to include the full range of language practices and skills that children in diverse communities had learned at home and brought with them to school. Dell Hymes, a linguist and ethnographer who was central to this endeavor, called for teachers to be involved in this work: Teachers "must in effect be ethnographers in their own situation. . . . It is the understanding and the insight of those in the concrete situation that will determine the outcome" (quoted in Cazden et al., 1972, p. xiv).

The presentation of cultural differences in Shirley Brice Heath's work and in her book entitled *Ways with Words* is now reasonably well known. Although the BTRS was somewhat diverse in terms of gender and race, we had not recognized the variety of ways human beings use language to communicate ideas. As for myself, I am a White female from a middle-class family and I had assumed that what I expected as competent and appropriate talk in school was both normal and the only correct form. It's difficult to overestimate the power back then of *Ways with Words* (Heath, 1983) for me, and for many others.

In it, Heath describes the social life and ways of using language, oral and written, in working class White and Black communities in the Carolina Piedmont area. Her book details how adults talk with children, when and where children talk with adults and with each other, storytelling practices and storybook reading, newspaper reading, and much more. Heath then contrasts these ways with words with the ways valued in school. She finds many important contrasts. For example, she points out the strength and power of the more metaphoric way of expressing ideas which the Black children she studied had learned in their homes and community. This was not what the teachers were generally looking for in early schooling; she suggested that it was a strength, and one that would become especially useful later on when more literary reading would be done—if the children were still engaged. Heath argues that the White working-class students she studied, on the other hand, were in this case accustomed to question-and-answer exchanges at home that were regularly focused on what exactly happened, on literal retellings, rather than on what an event or experience was like or similar to. She suggested that these students might do well in early schooling and in some other areas where this ability is appreciated, but these children might need additional help in developing the higher-level critical thinking and interpretation needed in later years. Heath describes the children in her study in detail—as she says, you come to know them. This view of language practices gave me a way to begin to see my own practices as cultural, that is, as not the only way.

With the BTRS I moved on to read a number of studies that focused on language practices in sharing time, the daily group meeting time in many early childhood classrooms. Sarah Michaels (1981) introduced the terms "topic-centered" and "topic associating" as ways to describe the differing styles that she heard children use to organize their sharing time accounts in one 1st grade. The former, associated largely with the White children in the classroom she studied, took the form of linear accounts with details supporting a clearly stated topic; the teachers then helped to expand these details where necessary and to improve general clarity with the audience in mind. Michaels suggested that this was preparation for the kind of explicit talking and writing required in school, where the audience and what they need to know may have to be imagined. The topic associating style that many of the Black children used had a less explicit topic and included many events or details with only an implicit thematic connection. Michaels presented an account of Deana, a Black girl who loved to share, and her travails trying to get her accounts "heard" in sharing time. She showed the different capacity of the teacher to understand the organization of this child's narrative and her consequent reduced ability to help her clarify or extend her ideas. Michaels, a White middle-class woman, herself tried to run sharing time once and, despite her own awareness of these styles, had trouble following narratives outside her own tradition. Michaels's stance, and Heath's as well, was that of an ethnographer, recording and describing social and linguistic life in great detail. Including elements both large and small, they functioned as participant observers—that is, they were doing research, but they also participated on occasion with the community or in the classroom. And they both cared deeply about the people being studied.

James Gee, a linguist, also tells a story of sharing time that informed my understanding significantly, this time of an African American child he calls Leona. As he analyzes Leona's failed attempt to be understood by her teacher, he focuses especially on the literary sophistication that Leona was able to employ in her story, this sophistication arguably a result of the many stories that she had heard in her home and community—that is, her membership in an African American culture of storytelling. To her teacher, again largely unaware of both this tradition and that there might be differences in storytelling styles, Leona was seen as a meandering storyteller, hogging attention, perhaps telling untruths—her competence and skill were overlooked. A hugely influential point for me in this article and in others was Gee's emphasis on the sophistication in Leona's storytelling. He was not only describing differences; nor was he describing differences that might need to be accommodated or acknowledged, perhaps remediated. Rather, he saw literary sophistication. This child spoke in Black dialect; her grammar was not mine, her way of moving from topic to topic was not what I would do in this context. And yet Gee argued that this child should be seen as at least competent and perhaps even "gifted" (Gee, 2015, p. 12).

As Steve Griffin, a BTRS member, wrote, recounting his experience of reading this literature and then trying to address what he learned there in his work as a 1st-grade teacher, "we began to see that we were not seeing the strengths" in some of our students (Griffin, 2004, p. 20).

This ethnographic research, and much more in this tradition that I also read, was directly pertinent to my work as a teacher. It was set in classrooms.

It involved relationships with students. Leona and Deana, as well as many of Heath's children, became children I felt I knew. By showing examples of other valuable ways of talking and expressing ideas, this work helped me to gain distance from my own. It gave me questions to ask, accustomed ways of doing things to probe. It opened up ideas of language variety in relation to thought and expression. The close analyses of talk in these studies gave me a method. I, like these ethnographers, began to make audio recordings in my classrooms and to take notes on talk.

Courtney Cazden's book *Classroom Discourse* came out in 2001. Cazden, a former teacher, but by then a professor at the Harvard Graduate School of Education, made the admirable and highly unusual move of returning to the classroom to teach 1st grade to see whether what she was teaching her teacher candidates actually worked. In doing this, she discovered many things, among them that as the teacher, she spoke two-thirds of the time—the children spoke only one-third. She and her co-researcher Hugh Mehan also made visible the common format of classroom discussion: initiation—response—evaluation—where the teacher would pose a question, a child would respond, and then the teacher would evaluate the response. Again, this was a case of naming something long assumed to be natural, as just the way to teach. However, once it was identified in this way, teachers could feel it when they did it, and then consider whether this format was always the best structure for their class discussion.

Other authors have continued this focus on instructional talk. Using transcripts of student and teacher talk, they point out additional ways that the conventions and culture of teaching define what counts as appropriate participation in classrooms and how the evaluations by teachers might miss unexpected, and often powerful, ideas and responses from students (e.g. Bang et al., 2012; Barnes, 1992; Delpit, 2012; Dutro, 2010; Dyson, 1992; Enciso, 2003; Furman & Traugh, 2021; González et al., 2006; Lee, 1995; Mayer, 2012; Park et al., 2015; Purcell-Gates, 1995; Warren & Rosebery, 1995). Douglas Barnes, a British educator who spent a great deal of time in classrooms and looked closely at the talk there, shined a light on what he called "exploratory talk," instances where children stumbled, seemed off topic or confused, occasionally halting, their thoughts not yet fully organized. Many of us might assume that these children were unsure or inarticulate, that they needed some help, but in his book *From Communication to Curriculum* (1992) he shared examples of student talk that demonstrated instead the role and value of this kind of uncertainty, which he called "first draft" talk, or "thinking out loud."

In response to these challenging ideas, in the BTRS we began to allow children more space to talk. We would wait longer than we used to. We might repeat what a student said in a questioning tone rather than evaluating it immediately. This move, which the scholars Mary Catherine O'Connor and Sarah Michaels (1993) have termed "revoicing," gives students the opportunity to expand or restate their thought, to agree or disagree with our rendition, meanwhile also giving ourselves, the teachers, the opportunity to think and to take notes on what was said in order to reflect later.

Here is Steve Griffin again, reflecting on how these ideas influenced his sharing time practices. Steve had audio-recorded his sharing time in response to his puzzlement about his student David. He wrote about this experience.

> "I've got a joke," says David, a handsome, seven-year-old African American boy. He smiles at his audience of classmates sitting on the floor before him, two months into their second-grade year. "Is it one of your long ones?" someone asks. "Yeah!" David replies. The audience shifts into more comfortable positions, settling in for a long story with obvious delight.
>
> During this performance, I, the teacher, remain unsettled. The unspoken, but firmly-rooted rules of sharing time have been toppled by a seven-year-old, and I'm not sure what I should do about it. Some of these rules, such as the appropriate length of a share and acceptable topics, were formed in the children's early years of schooling and came with them as they entered my second-grade classroom. Other rules were negotiated as this new class came into contact with my expectations and practices, for example, the acceptability of jokes as a topic for sharing time. I had agreed that we could share jokes. However, David's jokes did not fit into the category of jokes that I or his classmates expected. (Griffin, 2004, p. 22)

David's "jokes" were made-up stories which included the classroom community, adding characters from among his peers, commenting on their cool clothes, sometimes personalities, all in a humorous manner as part of his stories. He eventually began having his classmates act out parts of the story. In addition to being intrigued by the way David's stories seemed to strengthen the sense of community in his classroom, Steve attended to structural features of his storytelling; he became particularly interested in how close the story stayed to the central theme, how many detours it took and how these worked together. He could see David's narratives change and grow amid the needs and response of his audience. He saw that David chose his vocabulary carefully to increase the drama of his stories. Steve was able to see connections between David's jokes and his development as a writer more generally. Eventually, as Steve recounts, dramatic storytelling (what David called jokes) became a part of the classroom routine and an important part of the curriculum.

Vivian Paley's work joined us in this exploration as well (e.g., Paley, 1990). Like us, she was a teacher and, like the ethnographers, she audio recorded and then transcribed what the children were saying, exploring this record after the event. Unlike the ethnographers, Paley was generally less interested in cultural patterns and more interested in going deeply into the children's ideas. She emphasized the moral role of curiosity and connected a teacher's curiosity about students' ideas with the respect the children deserved for their thinking. She wrote movingly about her early reliance on the right answer as the way to know if she was teaching well. As she stepped back, allowing the children more space, Paley not only critiqued this earlier reliance but also often found that the ideas and questions she now heard from children challenged her own understanding. As she said with characteristic humor, "we only need to listen for our own errors and there is enough text to fill the school year" (Paley, 1990, pp. 48–9).

I too, as the following chapters will show, often found that the children's ideas pushed my own and deepened or challenged the right answers I thought I knew. I found that I was regularly taught particularly by those children who surprised me, whose responses seemed off or wrong. Because they were outside my expectations, these responses had the best possibility of helping me gain distance in order to see better both what I had been expecting and also, importantly, what value or interpretation the child was bringing instead. As the canaries in the coal mine helped the miners, these children often helped me see when the atmosphere was thin. But unlike the canaries, these children and their ideas, like Daniel in the introductory chapter, often helped me to find places where the atmosphere might be made more robust. The following chapters will show what I learned from them.

CONCLUSION

Paley and Cazden, and the ethnographic literature including the work of Michaels and Gee and Shirley Brice Heath and many others, were similar in their allegiance to very close-to-the-classroom investigations.

This research literature, and much more that I also read, I read as stories. I call them stories because I was able to imagine myself into these situations. They are accounts through which I met and got to know characters, saw teachers' moves and ideas and values. I was in conversation with this research, with these researchers, because their accounts were based on grounded and detailed accounts of teachers and children in the classroom. From them I gained, first, imagined experiences with a range of children and their talk and values, and second, a method by which to reflect on my own students' ideas and participation outside the busyness of the moment.

I too will tell stories. Each of the stories I will tell is the product of this learning. And like those from whom I learned, I base my stories on detailed observation including a range of details explored with as open a mind as possible in order to imagine the perspective of the participants. Stories, especially those with genuine detail, allow many interpretations. They do not lead to certainty. The texts that I include here do not represent final truths. With this work I ask you, the reader, to imagine yourself into the context, and to compare my context, my students, my curriculum, my experiences, with your own. These chapters do not contain any instructions to improve your teaching. My book is not on one side or another of the many debates engaging education. Its goal is to help you develop distance from assumptions about your practice and your students through experiencing imaginatively and in some detail my students and my practice and what I learned.

CHAPTER 2

Taking on the Stance

Practices of Teaching as Inquiry

Marilyn Cochran-Smith and Susan Lytle (1993) were among the first to theorize and describe teaching as inquiry; they called it "a stance" rather than a method of teaching. The use of this term reminds us that these inquiries are not over at some point—they do not result in final conclusions. *Nor do they result in rules or principles for teaching.* Instead, they are a continuous way of looking that emphasizes questioning and curiosity and continual reflection, and that can include both humor and distress. In this chapter I share the practices I have found useful for this work. After naming and explaining the practices, I will describe the induction of a new teacher researcher, JoAnn, into a group I was working with in order to give another view of the practices of teaching as inquiry.

Let me first highlight the three *principles that are the heart* of the practice of teaching as inquiry: curiosity, collegiality, and reflection.

VALUES OF INQUIRY

Curiosity

Nothing is more important than remaining curious about your students and their ideas. We educators encounter many categories and labels that seem to explain children's behavior, learning styles, and more. By remaining truly curious about children's ideas we can gain deeper knowledge, beyond such labels, knowledge of them as learners and as people, as well as more understanding of learning itself.

Collegiality

The second value is collegiality—having someone to talk to, to share stories with. I find myself sharing accounts of my puzzling moments, my laughter and occasional irritation, with a wide range of people, in both formal and informal contexts. You may notice that I include in my accounts many seemingly random conversations—sometimes with other teachers, but also with friends and family, the school secretary, the person down the street. Everyone may see things differently, notice what you don't, challenge what you assume.

Reflection

The third value is reflection. Reflection in the case of inquiry teaching means "stopping time" in order to reexamine first impressions of students and their ideas. This requires some record to aid recollection, what some call documentation. This might take the form of hastily written notes on what happened or what was said, an audio tape, student work. We call this "stopping time" because, with your documentation, you have halted the rapid pace of classroom life so that you can experience the moment, the event, more thoughtfully and more slowly.

PRACTICES

Now let us turn to more specifics of what a teacher researcher does in the classroom to enact these values.

Finding a Focus

Teaching involves many kinds of attention, many places to focus. What do we pay attention to in teaching as inquiry?

For myself, I usually focus my inquiries on what I have termed the "puzzling child." We might say the puzzling child is one who is struggling, or even failing, but I prefer to think of this child as one who puzzles me. Jillian (Chapter 8), for example, was presented to me as a child who was in trouble in academics and in behavior. In our reading group sessions, I began taking notes on her even before I really knew her. I believe these notes helped me to be curious about her rather than to just accept the description of her as a problem. The notes made visible some changes in her behavior over time that I otherwise might have missed. Most importantly, I believe she felt this attention and this interest and was strengthened by it on occasion.

Many teachers banded together to pay special attention to Haran. He was an 8th-grader who looked to be headed for separate special help classrooms in the high school and we hoped by our attention to give him a boost to perhaps change that prognosis. I jotted down his ideas as he participated in my reading group and then shared them, once a week, with the teachers' group. The others shared what they observed with me. Together we found areas of strength and of progress we might otherwise have missed. And Haran, in turn, began to talk about where he felt his troubles lay as he recognized our interest. He did manage to enter regular classes at the high school, and to graduate.

In other cases, it is moments of unexpected engagement or emotion that stand out for me and start me wondering and documenting and attending. "Why is so-and-so suddenly smiling so hard and at the same time insisting that I recognize that he talked to me in class?" "What are all these children talking so passionately about as they watch the clouds?" "Why such an unexpected misreading or mistake?" These are all questions I have pursued. I call them "puzzling moments" and they are often funny, although not always—they can sometimes be quite annoying as well. When I share such a moment with someone else to make them laugh, or to make them worry, or just to have them commiserate with me, that is often the beginning of more curiosity, about the child, or the group, or the book or idea, or all of the above. It often leads me to more regular, focused note-taking.

Rather than puzzles, sometimes teachers choose to explore particular curriculum structures, such as cooperative learning, the writing process, or guided reading; often in these cases the teacher has a bias in favor of these structures. It can be difficult to question what is going on in these well-regarded approaches. In cases of this sort, I have found it very useful to include a focus on a child for whom such practices are not going well. "Who is this not working for?" is an especially good question. Otherwise, we will explore the practice as if we assumed it was without problems or glitches. And, knowingly or not, we assume that any child who is not responding well is at fault, while, in fact, the child may have something to show us.

Jim Swaim, a BTRS member and 3rd grade teacher, had been frustrated by how the writing process, in particular the peer-editing part, was going in his classroom. He put audio recorders near some students while they were doing peer editing. He learned from listening to the recordings that the children's interpretation of what he was asking of them was not always exactly what he meant. Also, as he reflected on what they said, he realized that in fact he wasn't entirely sure himself what he meant: Is adding details always a good idea in writing? Where and when? How to know? He asked himself these questions as he explored the children's discussions in their peer-editing conferences. He changed aspects of his practice in response to what he heard and wrote a powerful article entitled "In Search of an Honest

Response" (Swaim, 2004). As is clear from his title, he was not finished questioning.

How to Stop Time: Taking Notes

Once you have a focus, or perhaps many foci, for your curiosity or concern, you need to develop forms of documentation that will work for you, that is, you need a way to *stop time* in order to keep the details of the child and the interaction in mind for later consideration. I generally take notes, scribbles really, as my students talk, and I save their written work.

I write key words as the students talk. Or sometimes I write nothing at all at the moment. In any case, I return again afterwords, either adding to my notes or writing fresh from recall. These notes are not exact. They do not include the pauses, the exact words an audio recording would get. I wish they were more exact, but they are the best I can do. I may rewrite them multiple times as I recall more.

I don't use a standard plan book because it doesn't have enough room for me to both write out my daily plan and take notes on what happened. As I look over what I have noted, I often asterisk what I see there that I should return to, what I notice that I need to clarify or discuss further with my students. In this way these notes are a major part of my planning.

You might think that you will not have time to write notes while children are talking, but I find that writing their ideas down during discussion can be one technique for establishing a reflective tone in the discussion. The children will notice your attention. They will occasionally slow down for you. They recognize that you are taking their thoughts very seriously. I also find that writing during a discussion keeps me from talking too much. I am busy, and so the children's ideas have more space to develop. As taking notes in this way becomes a habit, your memory grows. At first you sit down to write after a lively discussion, and you can remember nothing. Momentarily you panic. Then, as one child's remark comes to mind, others do too. You remember more and more. Also, the children can help you. They will usually be honored that you want to write down what they said. They will slow down during a discussion for this purpose or they will wait while you write. And if you have forgotten or are confused, ask the students. I have found that they often can remember, even much later, what they meant or what they said.

A final, very important benefit of writing is that it is a conversation with yourself. If you have colleagues or friends with whom you can share your observations, talk to them too. But writing is crucial, writing is part of your seeing and re-seeing the event. You ask yourself which word to use, what exactly happened. You make more sense and gain more distance from any assumptions or evaluations you have as you write.

If you can't find the time to write, I recommend speaking what you remember into your phone. You can't do this while you are teaching, of course, but if you practice you may find that you can recall what happened a little later on and dictate a record of some use.

Sticky Notes

Another form of documentation is sticky notes. In my reading groups, I sometimes ask my students as they read silently to write sticky notes on some question that I give them or just to write their reactions as they read. We may use them in writing a longer response later or we may share in the group, but, in addition, for me, having these notes and looking over them in quieter moments is often helpful in developing further insight into the student's responses. The notes shown in Figure 2.1 were taken when I asked my students to write a sticky whenever they were "struck-by" something as they read silently. I then took the stickies of each student and placed them in a line so that I could see what different individuals were responding to over time.

Notebook Dialogue

A third way to have documentation is to write back and forth with your students. Figure 2.2 shows a notebook conversation I had about the book *Stargirl* by Jerry Spinelli. This is a book about a very unusual girl, and about high school popularity and romance. As my students read silently, we would write back and forth to each other our reactions. These written dialogues took the place of my rapid scribbles during out-loud discussion, although, of course, we had those discussions too. In the page illustrated, I am asking my 5th-grade student, Leila, if she thinks that Stargirl, the character, is real or a myth. (In the book she is a remarkably unconventional character, sometimes her actions are well within the realm of possibility, other times less so.)

Leila replies, "How how, what kind of myth?" I was struck by her repeated "How? How?" She seemed so adamant. Later I wondered if she knew fully what I meant by "a myth." When I replied that I thought the character was teaching the reader, she disagreed—"I think she is just like that." This writing gave me immediate access to some of her feeling about the book and a sense of the way she was interpreting the character and engaging with her. It gave me as well various ideas for something to explore with her and the others later.

Figure 2.1. Children's Reading Response Sticky Notes

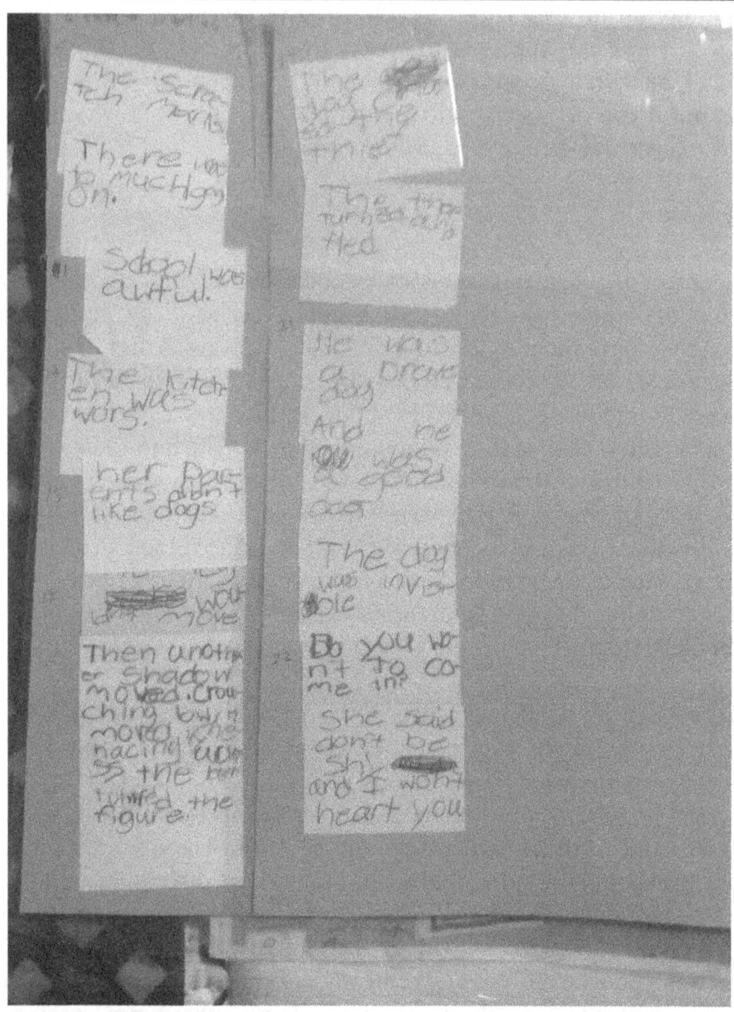

More Places to Observe

Observe everywhere you can. When you have found a child who puzzles you, joining that child during small group work allows you to focus in and write down details. In addition, notice particularly the situations where they are engaged, taking initiative or in some control. This could be on the playground, when arguing with another, in the art room. Or it could be in

Figure 2.2. Conversation Notebook, Thoughts on *Stargirl*

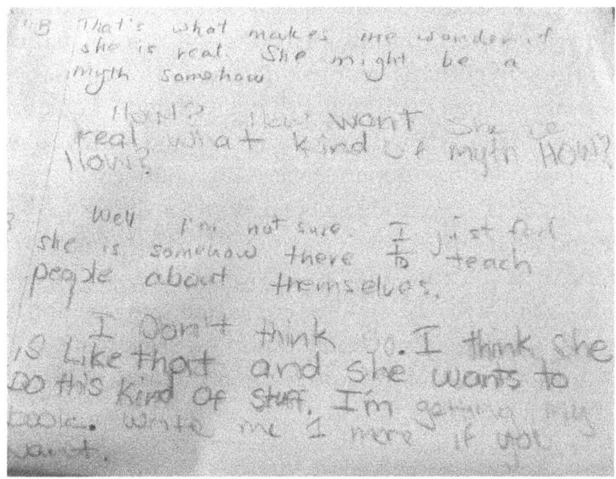

math class; but do not neglect moments that seem nonacademic. Attend to the ideas and the skills in use in these situations: How is language being employed? When the child is trying to make others laugh, is the use of language interesting, careful, unexpected, dramatic? Does this child make logical arguments when contesting a point in a game? Is the child a storyteller? Metaphoric thinker? Do they think out loud? How do these qualities vary with the context? You are looking for strengths. You are looking to see children as thinkers Thus, you will want to look in all situations and not ignore informal ones in favor of the ones where you have set the agenda.

A Caveat: Observation vs. Interpretation

I am regularly surprised in the seminars I teach for teachers by the categorical ways children are described to me by my very eager and reflective participants. Allan is described as a child with "processing problems." Another child was excluded from a practitioner research study by her teacher because the child "had no background knowledge." Students are categorized as visual learners, or as lacking confidence, needing more structure. The performance of an occasionally volatile 8th-grader was explained, "it's all about how she's feeling." Forming such categories is of course one of the principal ways humans navigate the world. We all do it. And yet such familiar ways of describing children, particularly puzzling children, while they may have some validity, quickly become fixed labels, much too simple for informing our understanding of the individuals in front of us. They impede our curiosity about all that is happening in the teaching–learning context. We needn't refuse our interpretations, but an interpretation or explanation like these must be a working hypothesis, an open question, an idea that you're developing and testing, not one that implies that it's all done. Look for discrepant moments—for example, when the overly active child is instead well-focused, when the child with little self-confidence seems confident.

To keep your curiosity strong, keep in mind the difference between what you observe and what you believe or assume. Try to stay with your observations. Try to stay away from any "fixes" for as long as you can, and from interpretations as to why the child is doing one thing or another. Instead, try to believe that the child is making important sense. This is not easy. We often revert to what we think we know about the student already, or about the type of student we think they are (see Bertrand & Marsh, 2015; Evans et al., 2019; Oláh et al., 2010).

One way to gain distance from what you assume is to gather a group of colleagues to read through your notes. Each participant takes on the role of one of the children. The group reads the notes or transcript out loud, each speaking the role of their assigned child. The discussion then opens with participants trying to describe the ideas and point of view of the child who was their focus. What could that child be thinking? This review by enactment focuses participants on the children's words. It keeps the group grounded there. It ensures that even students who said little receive a fair share of attention. Also, in focusing on the children's words, the read-through keeps the spotlight on them and off the teacher.

JOANN'S STORY

Let us look at JoAnn as she begins to take on an inquiry stance. She was part of a group of experienced teachers being introduced to these practices.

They had all been asked to choose a puzzling child. JoAnn chose Jose. Jose was a 2nd-grader whose life, according to the school, had been full of trauma. JoAnn told the group that he was a sad-looking child who had not been expected to do much in school. His teachers felt sorry for him. She said that he took very little initiative in his own learning, was passive, and lacked confidence.

Below are the notes JoAnn took on one occasion. She wrote down what she and Jose said and did and added teacher notes, comments to explain the context and to provide her own interpretations. These are labeled TN.

TN: We are taking a math test and Jose says he isn't feeling well.
TN: He is having a hard time focusing.
Teacher: Jose, what is wrong? Why are you not answering any questions?
TN: Jose shrugs and puts his head down.
Teacher: Do you want to talk about it? I can't help you unless you say something.
Jose: I just didn't sleep last night. I was up all night.
TN: He often uses excuses when he doesn't feel prepared for things or feels overwhelmed.
TN: We chat and then he sits down near me for the test.
TN: The only assistance he needs is reassurance and a multiplication table.
TN: No longer is he complaining about being sick or tired or anything. I think he is often overwhelmed and with his lack of confidence he just wants to have someone with him to reassure him that he is smart and doing great. Or just someone who cares.

She sees what she did as part of a relationship, which of course it is. But notice that when they are doing math she sets down only a summary, not a transcript, although she had made an earlier transcript about his feelings. What did he actually say about math? She does not tell us. Clearly, she assumed that the TLC was the important aspect of the discussion. Most teachers would agree. And JoAnn certainly helped Jose.

On the other hand, she did not explore any of his ideas; we don't know what he actually said. Herein lies one crucial problem, I believe. Many of us, well-intentioned and concerned about children who are struggling, do not explore adequately the sense that the children are making. What was he thinking? Are we missing his ideas? The claim of teacher research is that indeed we are. JoAnn is not necessarily wrong about what Jose needed, but in addition, and perhaps crucially, he needed to be respected as a thinker. As teacher researchers our moral commitment is to believe that the child has mathematical ideas.

In a later example, Jose's teacher brought together a small reading group that she believed would allow Jose to participate. This time I asked her to audiotape the interaction. After a picture walk through *Thunder Cake* by Patricia Polacco (1990), exploring the story through its dramatic illustrations, they previewed vocabulary they would need as they read it.

Teacher: What is the next word?
Jose: Thunder.

Teacher: What does *thunder* mean?
Jose: Hawks shoot up in the air. A flash of light in the sky.
Teacher: Jose, think about what you just said, what do you think you are describing?
Jose: I know, I know, can I do the next word?
Teacher: Yes.
Teacher: Peter, what is thunder?
Peter: A boom in the sky.
Teacher: Good answer.
Chan: No, *thunder* is when the air moves and makes a loud sound.
TN: Then Chan reads the definition in the glossary.
Teacher: What is the next word? [this one is lightning]
Jose: A flash of light in the sky. That sometimes hits you.
Teacher: What is the flash?
Edward: Electricity. It is very powerful.
Teacher: Have you ever heard how to tell how far away a storm is?
Peter: You count between the thunder and lightning.
Chan: No, the lightning is first, light is faster than sound.
Teacher: Yes, you count after you see the lightning and stop when you hear the lightning. What does it mean?
Mike: How far away the storm is. When you count to 3 that means it is 3 miles away. You can tell if the storm is going away.

JoAnn shares this transcript with the group. In her introduction to the transcript, she explains "it is a spirited and informative conversation, a typical Monday discussion before reading our weekly story. Jose has participated which is great. He appears pleased with his contribution."

Participation is something I often hear teachers praising. Most of us would agree that we enjoy it when children become engaged and enthusiastically participate. But, again, is the teacher really engaging with what the child is saying? As JoAnn shares the conversation in our class of experienced teachers, other teachers notice the odd moment when Jose offers "hawks fly up" as a definition for *thunder*. Is he imagining the hawks flying up? Where does that image come from? It feels less like a definition than an actual experience. Then he says "a flash of light in the sky" for *lightning*, and he mentions that lightning might hit you. The book has some dramatic pictures, and he has done a picture walk ahead of reading the book and seen them. It occurs to the group as we look over his words that when he says "hawks fly up" as a response to thunder, one might see Jose as responding in a very artistic manner, a dramatic way. He has perhaps seen something like this, the group suggests, and it has stayed with him. His statement about lightning is also like this—dramatic. He feels the danger, perhaps.

JoAnn responds that in fact he is an artist—that is his strength. She had thought of this talent only in connection with Jose's drawing, but she sees it now in this response to the story. She feels she had missed it in the actual moment.

I am sharing this because I want to demonstrate that a very good teacher like JoAnn can fail to recognize good ideas and strong intellectual participation from this child, perhaps because she feels sorry for him and also because she has some explanations for him ready at hand—disorganized family, lack of self-confidence. We all do this! And yet, upon stopping for reflection, using (in this case) an audio recording of the conversation to ground us in what happened and was said rather than in our assumptions, we can see, with the help of discussion with others, that Jose has in fact demonstrated some skills that are very much a part of how we hope all children will read literature.

Other notes, as the year goes on, reveal that he does take initiative, contrary to the initial assumption—in fact he questions other children on their ideas; we learn that his family spends time outdoors and he has experiences of this to share, and more. As a group, we pore over his writing, where we notice that he is developing a humorous and lively style. Jose may indeed deserve sympathy, but, at the same time, over the course of JoAnn's study, more examples of Jose's dramatic and visual response to the books he was reading came to light. Jose went through the year speaking out more and more, demonstrating his knowledge of nature, and translating that into funny and increasingly well-constructed writing.

Through including note-taking, audio recording, and later reflection in her daily teaching, JoAnn went beyond her original idea. She became more broadly curious about what Jose was thinking and how he responded. Over time, he emerged, for her, and also, crucially, for himself, as a thinker and an engaged participant in the classroom.

I leave this chapter with a final quotation from a friend, a teacher and a writer, Alexandra Miletta:

> **Teaching . . . requires an inner strength, both to persist through initial difficulties, and to resist the growing tide of simplistic labels and problematic use of data. You must first and foremost have faith in your curiosity, your desire to know children and to recognize their fascinating ways of coming to know and understand their world.**
>
> —Alexandra Miletta, 2024

Part II

READING WITH CHILDREN

CHAPTER 3

Reading Achievement and Book Talk

I have been a reading teacher for many years in a large urban district. I teach students from a diversity of backgrounds. Some children come to school already intimately involved with books. They relax right into read-alouds and are eager to learn to read for themselves. But many of the children I teach do not appear to be so engaged. Many reasons for this lack of engagement are put forward. Many educators and educational researchers focus on family literacy and a lack of reading in the home as the cause; others take a broader view and blame aspects of the social and economic situation that parents and children inhabit. Others blame instruction, too much phonics, too little phonics, the wrong books, poorly trained teachers, and so on.

After a long list of areas in which a child may need more help in order to read well, Catherine Snow, a Harvard expert in reading and language, acknowledges in a major report on reading commissioned by the RAND Corporation, that among the most important factors in reading success or failure is how a child feels about their strength as a thinker in school (Snow, 2002).

To me, this is a tremendously significant claim. As stated earlier, the commitment of this work is to the idea that all children are thinkers. But Catherine Snow's observation based on her research, and seconded by my own experience, suggests that the ideas and responses of many of our students are not taken seriously or they are not heard at all. These students are not responded to as thinkers by their teachers and so they do not feel their "strength as thinkers." The following accounts will address this concern.

Let me begin by noting that it is not easy to be curious and reflective in busy classrooms. We have lesson plans to follow. There is not a lot of time. In addition, many areas of instruction, including reading, have become more and more bound to scripts and predetermined objectives. As teachers, we are making fewer of our own decisions and thus are less and less able to grant student responses the curiosity and the attention they deserve.

The following lesson plan was made by one of my best young student teachers.

> I will begin by reminding the students about the strategies we are using to think about characters.
>
> 1. thinking about what a character says and does,
> 2. looking at both the words and the pictures,
> 3. trying to infer a character's feelings,
> 4. making predictions,
> 5. noticing if a character changes over the course of the story,
> 6. making connections to characters using your own experiences.
>
> I will continue reading. On the third spread, I will stop and ask, "Can we infer what Jeremy thinks about Antonio?" On the next spread, I will stop and ask, "What is he thinking about doing?"

And so it goes on. Her goal here was clearly that children should come to understand and connect with Jeremy, a character in this book, and that they should practice the ways of coming to know characters that they have been taught.

This kind of teaching is intended to make explicit for the students, particularly for students who may not like to read and/or may not be successful at it, many of the things we think that good readers do intuitively. It is intended to level the playing field between children who "just know" how to engage with books and to enjoy them, and children who don't have this ease.

I believe I gained a good deal from encountering and incorporating some of these ideas and practices into my work. They made many aspects of comprehension and response explicit in ways they had not been before. I in no way intend to abandon these practices. But I think there is a downside to the certainty contained in these kinds of lists and sets of objectives and goals. The efficiency and clear focus expressed here blind us to the many unexpected ways people interact with literature. The very clarity of this planning diminishes our curiosity; it obstructs our view of our students' thinking and thus our ability to support them in feeling themselves as thinkers.

Unlike the children in such a tightly controlled lesson plan, the students you will see in the following accounts were not only trying to guess what was in the teacher's mind, but also to articulate what was in their own. I think that you will see these students exhibit a strength in sticking to their own ideas as well as a seriousness about applying literature to their own lives.

In cases where it is relevant I will also include some small accounts of the direct instruction in vocabulary and decoding that I provided—of course this is a part of teaching reading and it would not be a fair portrait without some sense of this part of the process, particularly in this time where reading is portrayed as all one approach or all another, rather than in its true complexity.

The next three chapters will each tell the story of very good books being read and discussed by different groups of students. I hope you will see what I saw in reviewing the notes I took as the students read and talked, particularly the notes I took on those moments where the students surprised me, what I call "puzzling moments." I was regularly surprised by the depth of the students' responses when they were given room to discuss what was on their minds. My own later reflections on their ideas helped me to develop a better picture of how the students were using literature I brought to them to think about their lives. I was able to connect more thoughtfully with their ideas and intentions and thus to support their view of themselves as thinkers who will incorporate literature and learning into their lives.

CHAPTER 4

"So Cold"

Reading *Maniac Magee*

I learned a great deal from this 6th-grade book group about these students as individuals and about their friendship. However, in addition, this group challenged me to a deeper understanding of how we respond to literature more generally. This challenge came largely from the puzzling child in the group whose responses often contrasted with my own.

The group was organized around Darius. Darius was an African American 6th-grader whose family still maintained some connections to family in the West Indies. His mother worked for the city as an administrative assistant. Darius, an active and imaginative child who didn't sit still easily, was very proud of his family and his background. He was also a boy who didn't like to read; he was reading a bit below grade level by the formal and informal assessments we used. For these reasons, his teacher asked me to make up a reading group for him. I allowed him to include his two friends, Mike and Stan, both accomplished and enthusiastic readers. Stan's family was White, Mike's mixed White and African American. In both of their families the parents held professional jobs and had college degrees. I include these details because many ethnographers, for example Shirley Brice Heath (1983) and Lisa Delpit (1988), have found that the larger the differences in social class and professional and educational experience between student and teacher, the more difficult it can be for the teacher to understand the student's strengths and approaches. This distance may have played a role in the puzzles that Darius presented to me.

EPISODES

The following narratives are based on notes I took on what my students said. I wrote quickly as we talked and later added points as I remembered them. I wrote down mainly what puzzled me and so my notes don't cover all that we did or talked about. And, as usual, I also mentioned what I found puzzling to other teachers or other people; I regularly learned something from these conversations, both formal and informal.

The book I chose to read with this group was *Maniac Magee* by Jerry Spinelli. *Maniac Magee* is a hard book in many ways. It is full of metaphor. It takes an odd humorous tone at times that can be hard for many students to pick up. It is an uncommon mixture of true and fictional details, a wildly improbable account of running away combined with a historically situated presentation of racial disharmony.

Maniac's parents have died in a trolley crash, and he is living with his difficult aunt and uncle, from whom he runs away. Maniac is an innocent. A White boy, he runs into the Black neighborhood of a segregated city without any awareness of racial strife; there he learns about prejudice, he helps others and is helped, and he encounters hostility as well as friendship.

The range of realistic and unrealistic details suggested to me that we make a list of what could be true and what seemed unlikely. The boys said that the fact that his family evidently does not search for him after he runs away was unrealistic, as were the ideas that he sleeps in a zoo near the buffalos, and that he eats dinner with a family with so many children they apparently don't notice that he is there. Racism, which also appears in the book, is true, the boys said. Maniac's ability to untie very difficult knots, and that he ran away, were both considered realistic ideas.

Because Darius loved to draw, I incorporated a good deal of drawing in our work, particularly organized around the metaphoric language. We drew the way that the flapping tongue of Maniac's old shoe is compared to a dog's tongue, how a book falling down looked like a bird with open wings, and so on. The book was fun and funny, and the group enjoyed it. But it had dark moments too.

1. Who's Shouting at Maniac?

In the part of the city where he has arrived, Maniac eventually gets to know a Black family, the Beales. When they realize that he is homeless, they take him in. He feels comfortable and, as Spinelli writes, "Maniac loved almost everything about his new life. But everything did not love him back" (p. 56). There were those who told him to return to his own kind. One day he returned to the Beales' home to find "fishbelly," a reference to his Whiteness, written on their steps. Things escalate and he feels he must leave the Beales' home for their sake. Disconsolate, he walks out of town. On both sides of the street as he walks are kids, yelling. The Blacks are on one side and the Whites on the other. Perhaps they begin by yelling at Maniac or cheering him for having untied a particularly difficult knot, it's unclear, but soon the two sides are snarling and yelling at each other.

> ***Me:*** I'm liking it less well. This part is painful.
> ***Mike:*** They're cheering Maniac Magee on as he runs down the middle [between the two sides of town].
> ***Stan:*** No, I don't think so. It's different. Both sides are bad to each other. I was surprised that both sides were bad.

[Kids reread to check]

> ***Mike:*** They each treat the other bad, then they get back at the other. You can't really say how it started.
> ***Me:*** Well, I guess slavery started it.
> ***Mike:*** Yeah, I was going to say that, but I didn't want to be mean.
> ***Me:*** You worried that Stan and I would feel bad?
> ***Mike:*** Yes.
> ***Me:*** Well, we have to be able to talk about these things.
> ***Stan:*** And now racism is past.
> ***Darius:*** [Darius thinks before he answers] Well, there's an 8th-grader who's a racist.
> [Tells a story I couldn't quite understand]

This part of the book is truly painful. I am struck by how thoughtful Mike is, not wanting to hurt Stan or me. And I am surprised that he misread it initially, although I too had difficulty, and had to look carefully to understand this. As Stan says, it is unexpected—you expect one group to side with Maniac. The Whites, I guess. Or perhaps you expect one side to be in the right. Maybe the Blacks. But instead, two crowds are yelling at each other, "an ugly, snarling black-and-white escort" for Maniac as he walks out of town.

Mike tries to protect the White participants, Stan and me, from blame. Stan tries to comfort us all, saying that racism is past. Darius thinks and says, not entirely. I am impressed with their conversation, their joint attempt at understanding their world.

The book goes on.

After leaving the Beales—for their own good, as he sees it—Maniac has found a home with an old man, Grayson, an employee at the zoo where Maniac had been sleeping since leaving the Beales. Maniac is trying to teach

Grayson to read while enjoying the stories Grayson tells of his early days trying to break into the Major Leagues as a pitcher.

Again, difficulties arise in the story and we react in different ways.

2. So Cold

One day, after the boys had been asked to read a few chapters as homework, I ran into Mike in the library early in the day. Rather than even saying hello, he looked at me, with a very sad, almost disbelieving expression. "Grayson died," he said.

Later that day, as we were together in our book group, we all read what happened next. Grayson had died in his sleep, and, having lost Grayson, Maniac is homeless once more. In despair he runs again and eventually finds himself in the National Park at Valley Forge, Pennsylvania, where George Washington's army suffered through what Spinelli describes as the "vast, dark, frozen desolation" of a terrible winter during the Revolutionary War. Maniac sleeps in one of the huts that Washington's army used, or actually a replica built by the National Park. In a very disturbing scene, Spinelli writes, Maniac lay down, "dreams pursued memories, courted and danced and became one with them, and the gaunt beseeching phantoms that called to him had the rag-wrapped feet of Washington's regulars. . . . In that bedeviled army there would be no more recruits. No one else would orphan him . . . he waited for death" (p. 123).

We read on. During the second night as he waits to die, Maniac hears the voices of some small children coming from another of the huts; he drags himself outside to see what is going on. He finds some young runaways, two little boys who think they are going all the way to Mexico. Maniac was about to die, but now he realizes the danger these children are in, and he tricks them into coming with him so that he can take them back to their home.

At this point, I asked my students: "Wow, a big change. What do you think saves Maniac here?"

> ***Mike:*** I think [the little kids] make him want to help them and that saves him.
>
> ***Darius (speaking slowly, looking down):*** So cold around him.
>
> ***Stan:*** He's first dying, then coming to life.

Mike and Stan gave the answers I would give. Helping others, being needed, helps Maniac return to life. That's what I expected to hear. They saw a connection between helping the little boys and returning to life.

Darius's answer, however, was different; he spoke slowly, saying "so cold." Altogether it surprised me. I was wondering, why does he talk about the cold? I was puzzled. Was Darius responding this way because he was deficient in Mike and Stan's understanding? This was my initial feeling. I wrote down what he said and kept my puzzlement in mind.

3. McNab House

I noticed another similarly puzzling response a few days later. In this part of the book, Maniac is returning the runaway boys to their home. Once there he finds that their family, the McNabs, is racist and generally dysfunctional. The boys are not treated well. They don't go to school regularly. They are allowed to drink and smoke and swear; the house is filthy, and the language and racist ideas of the family are also filthy.

Spinelli writes, "Now there was no room that Maniac could stand in the middle of and feel clean. Now there was something else in that house, and it smelled worse than garbage and turds. He ran far that day, away from the town, letting the wind wash him" (p. 153).

I was struck by the metaphoric use of the wind washing, and probably I also wanted to make sure that the boys understood it, and so I said, "I wonder why Maniac needed to let the wind wash him."

The boys respond:

Darius: Beer, urine.
Stan: Racism.
Mike: Racism.
Darius: Yeah, and every time he [John McNab] says bad things about blacks, he [Maniac] thinks of the Beales.

Again, Stan and Mike said what I would have said, and Darius said something I would not. In my notes for that day, I wrote: "Beer or urine as striking as racism?!" Darius spoke rather slowly, "beer, urine"; he seemed almost to be in the smelly room.

After the other boys offered the answer "racism," the answer that I would have given to my question, Darius said, "Yeah, and every time he [John McNab] says bad things about blacks, he [Maniac] thinks of the Beales." On second thought, I saw that maybe he was agreeing with the others—he does say "yeah"—but what was this about the Beales? In the book, the Beales are a paragon of home and parenting. As I said, this Black family took Maniac in when they realized he was homeless. But what Darius said here is not in the book. It doesn't say that when the racist McNabs said terrible things about Blacks, Maniac thought about the Beale family. Why did Darius suggest that? Had he not read well? This event stayed in my mind. I shared my puzzlement with a teacher of West Indian background whom I knew. Her response was deeply informative. "That's what we do," she told me, "When people say bad things about our people, we think of good examples." So, it appears, if this woman is right, that Darius may have not only understood the racism in the book but felt it deeply enough to need to respond by thinking of the Beales himself, or, alternatively, he felt Maniac deeply enough that he was suggesting that Maniac do this.

4. Letters

When students are very engaged in a book, one activity that I enjoy is writing letters to the characters. Darius chose to write a letter to Amanda Beale, the character who led Maniac to her family and eventually become his friend.

> Dear Amanda Beale,
>
> Hello! Your mom is wicked nice. I could believe that your brother and sister are annoying but they seem nice, your dad is nice, your dog is nice and you're nice. You have a nice family and I will be glad to visit you. I'm sorry about what happened to your book that you lended to Maniac. Mars Bar acted like a real jerk. But you are a caring, intelligent girl and I honestly think your future will turn out great for you,
>
> Sincerely, D.

The other kids teased Darius when they read his letter because they said they could tell by it that he had a crush on Amanda Beale. Darius was embarrassed; he seemed to acknowledge his crush. I was thrilled—a crush on a literary character. How great!

Later, when the boys were discussing the color line that Maniac had innocently crossed in the story, Stan, taking on the persona and writing as a Black character named Mars Bar, wrote to Maniac advising him that he had a lot to learn about the Black–White divide. Darius then took on the task of writing a reply to Mars Bar (Stan really) as if he were Maniac: "I disagree that I have a lot to learn about the black white divide. I knew it was divided for a reason so there wouldn't be a lot of death. I understand that whites should stay on the white side and blacks on the black side." To me, Maniac did have a lot to learn; but Darius, perhaps less so. Perhaps he was really writing as Darius, giving his own thoughts. I don't know. It seems a considered answer based on a felt sense of what could happen.

REFLECTIONS

As I puzzled over these moments, I began to see that Darius was deeply in the book. He felt the cold, the smells of urine, of beer. He liked Amanda. He felt the racism in the McNab household so much that he turned his thoughts to the Beales. Clearly Darius's ability to connect with literature was strong and vital; he was able to forge useful and supportive connections to reach an understanding. And yet at first I had felt that his approaches to literature, and perhaps in other areas of schooling, were less useful, less powerful than those of others.

As I noticed the visceral quality of his initial responses, and began to appreciate it, I came to see that I often moved my students out of the situations depicted in books into an analytical place, asking them to respond fairly immediately in more distanced ways. I was continually asking for a wrap-up term, some sort of idea that applied not just to this event but more generally. He comes back to life by helping others; it is the racism in the McNabs' home that makes him feel dirty. In my questioning, I was trying, without really knowing it consciously, to move the boys out of the real situation and the feeling associated with it and into an explanatory principle. I was looking for a response distanced from the situation being described. And so when Darius stayed with the situation, feeling the cold, smelling the urine, I thought Darius was not seeing the larger point. When I have shared these small transcripts with other teachers, they typically see Darius very much as I did. A number have suggested that he is perhaps developmentally unable to do yet what the other boys are doing.

This reminds me of a story told to me by a graduate student I once taught, a woman originally from Uganda. She had been part of a seminar where every student was asked to bring in a book to read with the others. She brought in a book about the genocide in Rwanda among the Hutus and the Tutsis. As she led the discussion of this book, she was shocked by how quickly the American students wanted to move to causes, for example, to colonialism, to economics, how quickly they moved out of the horror of the actual event. I was doing something similar. I too was moving my students out of the situations depicted in books into an analytical place asking them to respond fairly immediately in more distanced ways. Why would I do this? I now wonder. It seems to me that a real appreciation of literature should not privilege the abstract, the distanced, emotional engagement and, in this case, pain. Darius was an important teacher for me.

> **The teacher is no longer merely the one-who-teaches, but one who is himself [sic] taught in dialogue with the students, who in turn while being taught also teach.**
>
> —Freire, 1993

CHAPTER 5

Is *There's a Boy in the Girls' Bathroom* Fiction?

This next story revolves around a 6th-grader as well. Again, at first, I missed the point of what the child was understanding due to my own certainty that the answer I was expecting was the only answer. Fortunately, like Darius, the child was stubborn, and I had my notes on what happened, and colleagues with whom to discuss them. Again, I ended up learning something new, about the child and in this case, about the book too.

Cesar spoke Cape Verdean Creole at home with his parents, where there were many signs of economic and emotional stress. He had been in the United States for most of his life and spoke conversational English reasonably well, although many common expressions and metaphoric uses stymied him: for example, in my notes I see that he asked me the meaning of the expression, "what have we here?"; he didn't know what a flea market was; he was astonished that it was good English to say "the wind whipped around the corner." These common expressions in English are not ones we usually teach, and so it was good that he was able to ask me, and it was no wonder that he tended to have trouble comprehending the books he read.

Overall, he was not an engaged student. He rarely did his homework, failed the state tests, and was considered to be a very slow learner, as well as a concrete thinker. His 6th-grade teacher often sent him to me during his classroom's independent reading time because otherwise he would disrupt his entire class. He asked me once, with real intensity, "Why do people like to read?"

After a number of books he didn't really engage with, I decided to give him *There's a Boy in the Girls' Bathroom* by Louis Sachar to read. A lot of books for children are not literature—but this one, I believe, is. It is a very good book about a boy named Bradley who does poorly in school and is regularly in trouble and has no friends. A counselor named Carla tries to help Bradley, and the story revolves around them and their relationship as well as Bradley's attempts to learn about friendship. Cesar too saw the school counselor and his behavior was not always acceptable in the classroom.

I usually saw Cesar alone, because in groups he had consistently proven to be very distracted. He read very slowly. Generally, I would read a few paragraphs and then he would take over reading outloud to me. I could hear that he continued to make small errors as he read, "the" for "and," "for" for "from," and often missed verb tense markers. To help him correct himself, I often would reread the sentence as he had spoken it, including the small error he had made, and ask him to find what seemed off. Sometimes I read it his way and then the correct way and asked him which he thought was better; he usually answered this correctly. In order to direct him to attend to small words, and to help him become aware of them, I copied pages from the book and then blacked out the prepositions in cases where they were predictable—for example, I ran [] the house—and asked him to tell me what word I had blacked out. This was easy for him even though his ability to notice which preposition worked was not strong when he read out loud. I wondered, Was the problem his ear for English, his ability to decode, too much to think about at once, or was he rushing and not paying attention? Maybe a combination. He showed some progress in these activities and in any case enjoyed them.

We began to read *There's a Boy in the Girls' Bathroom* using these techniques. After a number of sessions, it became clear that Cesar was beginning to enjoy *There's a Boy in the Girls' Bathroom.* Eventually I felt able to suggest that he take the book into his classroom for their Independent Reading times. He still came in for our more focused sessions, though, and one day when he arrived, I asked him what chapter he was now on: "Eleven," he said. I started to open my book to 11, and he laughed. "You think I would be on 11?! I'm on 21." He was proud of his progress. His teacher reported that he was now able to read silently in the classroom. Finally, a book he liked!

The following episodes, developed from my scribbled notes, gave me insight into how he was experiencing the book and what connections he made to it.

EPISODES

1: Why Doesn't Bradley Say "I"?

I had been leading a discussion in Cesar's classroom about first- and third-person narratives. I asked the students to switch sentences from first to third person, and then asked them to tell me in what person the book that they were reading was written. Cesar did not participate in our discussion until, late in the discussion, he raised his hand and asked in a deeply wondering tone, "Why doesn't Bradley say 'I'?"

I remember that I lamely explained again the grammatical difference between third and first person, but later I continued to think about the intensity of his question. I can still see his face as he asked it. The book is written in the third person. And yet it is from the main character's perspective. I realized that any reader, Cesar included, would be deep into the perspective and thought process of this main character, named Bradley. As a reader, you feel like you know Bradley from the inside. Cesar was bringing up something I should have included in my lesson. Cesar's experience of Bradley's inner life made the issue of first person and third person so much more vivid. And, most important to me, it showed that he was following the book with emotion and concentration.

2: "It's Not Fiction"

A week or so later I was teaching a very standard lesson on genre in the same classroom. This concept was old hat to most of these students, but it is a lesson that sometimes leads to interesting discussion when books do not clearly fit into one genre or another. I also often relied on it as an easy way for me to find out what they were reading during their independent reading times. Together, we categorized some books we all knew as either fiction or nonfiction. We noted some subcategories: science fiction, realistic fiction, fantasy, etc. Then the students took turns stating what they were reading independently and how they would categorize it. Everything went smoothly until we came to Cesar.

Cesar told me that *There's a Boy in the Girls' Bathroom* was nonfiction. We stopped. The other students remonstrated. They told him it could be real, but it was not. There could be a boy like Bradley, but there was no such boy. They were very nice and very clear, but Cesar did not move an inch. He just disagreed. He said repeatedly that the book was true, nonfiction. As the others kept trying to explain, at last he said, "Okay," and we waited. "Maybe the story happened to the author's son, not the author." That was as far as he was willing to go. I was stunned. What to do?

Cesar himself had trouble behaving in school and was seeing a counselor. He had personal experience to bring to bear on the events and descriptions in the book, and he believed this book. And yet it was fiction, and he was not able to see this. I returned to the book without much idea what to look for—just browsing, wondering. But soon enough I began to see something.

You may know those moments when you are reading a book and you say to yourself, this really happened—this isn't the author's art or imagination, this really happened to the author. I have been struck by this feeling in many books, I think most often in children's literature. I think these moments are visible because the description is unusually detailed, maybe more detailed than seems quite necessary, and at the same time the event is unexpected. Beverly Cleary describes Ramona and her friend, Howie, smashing bricks with great satisfaction on a series of summer days. To me that does not feel "made up." I have always believed that that must have really happened. As Cesar might say, either Cleary did it herself as a child or one of her children did. *A Boy in the Girls' Bathroom* is unusually full of these moments. Once you begin to notice them, it is quite striking.

Then I looked up the author. I learned that he had married a school counselor. He wrote the book soon after their marriage. In addition, he used her real name in the book, Carla. Why would he do that? Cesar is on to something. This author is trying especially hard to be true to something in his life. It may be fiction, but it also appears to be true. I gained a lot of insight into the book from Cesar; he showed me things I had not seen in it. Above all, I had increased respect for the quality and energy of his reading.

Later on in the week, I decided to give Cesar some printed books to sort. He put *There's a Boy in the Girls' Bathroom* in with *Because of Winn-Dixie*. They were all stories, he said.

FINALE

The story could end here. But it did not—it deepened for me when, a few days later a boy, Devin, came into my room crying, telling me he had no friends; he had had a fight on the playground and was very upset. Cesar was there finishing his reading time with me while I tried to console Devin—although I was not successful at all. When I had to leave after a few minutes, Cesar asked if he could stay with Devin. He was so serious and insistent that, after trying to talk him out of it a few times, I finally let him. My officemate, who agreed to supervise them from her desk at the other end of the very large room, overheard and then scribbled down notes for me of an extraordinary conversation. Cesar listened to Devin explain how he was feeling, asked for clarification and responded with thoughtful suggestions, many of which appeared to derive from the book.

Devin asked, "How do you make friends?"

Cesar replied: "It's hard. I have lots of friends in this school. It's easy for me now because I've been in the school for 11 years." Cesar tried to get

Devin to name a friend, but Devin didn't seem to have any. Cesar then said, "I'm your friend." (This is what the counselor in the book said to the character Bradley. It is an odd thing for a counselor to say, and an odd thing for a 6th-grade boy to say to a younger boy he barely knows.)

Cesar then questioned Devin about whether he liked sports, or pizza, or candy, seemingly searching for a connection that might help Devin to make friends. When he got nowhere with this strategy, he commented, "I used to have a stuffed animal and he was my friend." And then he asked, "Do you have a lot of stuffed animals?" Devin acknowledged that he did.

Stuffed animals were the recourse Bradley had in the story—he named them and played out, and improved upon, his daily dramas using them; he called them his friends. The conversation continued with Cesar getting Devin to describe his stuffed animals, what they were like and how some were scary. Throughout, Cesar was very sympathetic and very engaged, according to my officemate. She was amazed.

FINAL REFLECTIONS

The first challenge of teacher research is to uncover the ideas of the puzzling child. The next task, if you truly honor a child as a thinker, is to ask, Can you teach other children from this child's ideas? Did this child, Cesar—a child from a poor family whose parents did not get far in school, a child who fits the profile of a child who might not succeed in school—does he, in fact, have something to teach other children about literature, something that might even be on the tests?

Of course he does.

Cesar was determined to tell us, when he refused to accept that the book was fiction, that the author was writing with unusual honesty, and was staying very true to his experience. He had noticed that there were books he could trust—where the depiction of character and event was serious, where he could use his reading in real life. We could learn from Cesar. How did he know that there was something different about Sachar's writing here? What were the clues? Can we all learn to make these judgments about other books? We could also wonder with Cesar why Bradley does not say I—why is this book in the third person? Cesar could lead us into many areas of literary discussion. He deserves to shine.

Further, I think that Bradley's loneliness, and his bad behavior, were things Cesar could respond to. He perhaps recognized some ways that his counselor had helped him and understood how the counselor in the book helped Bradley. He had made a strong and complex imaginative connection with a literary character. And he then brought this to bear on his conversation with Devin.

Cesar reminds us how the right book can articulate your experience for you, make it almost more real, how a book you love becomes a part of your real life and how a book, especially when you are young, can teach you about sympathy and feeling for others.

EPILOGUE

One morning, I was standing next to the principal as the kids streamed in. When Cesar went by, the principal mentioned that he had discussed some of the difficulties in that boy's home with him. Cesar told him that, when things got loud and angry there, he comforted his younger brother, in the same way that his older brother had comforted him—by taking him into another room and shutting the door. After hearing this, and recalling how Cesar had helped Devin, I arranged for Cesar to help in the kindergarten. He, who was often seen by teachers as a rough child, was wonderful with these children and helped them with their reading and thus of course helped himself as well.

CHAPTER 6

Reading *Crash*

Readers, of course, bring their own experiences to the books they read, and doing so is a way for them to come to understand the book. However, we are less likely to take seriously the comments and concerns that a good book brings up for students when they focus, or seem to, not on the book, but on themselves.

This chapter tells the story of four 8th-grade boys who use a book to talk about themselves and the world they find themselves in. They are discussing, I believe, what Maxine Greene calls "the themes of their existence":

> Curriculum ought to provide a series of occasions for individuals to articulate the themes of their existence and to reflect on those themes until they know themselves to be in the world and can name what has been up to then obscure. (Greene, 1978, pp. 18–19)

These four boys had been sent to me for small group reading because they were reading below the norm to varying extents. They were a particularly diverse group: Lim was from Cambodia, Mohammad was North African, Carlos was from the Dominican Republic, and Reynaldo was from Brazil. They each spoke their first language as well as very competent English and were not receiving any services for English as a second language. The book we read was *Crash* (1997) by Jerry Spinelli. This book tells the story of a middle-schooler who is nicknamed Crash because of his aggressive and headstrong personality. My recounting is based on notes I took at the time or right after our reading group sessions. I wrote down, as I usually do, those moments where the students were especially serious or engaged and when they surprised me. I'll share my notes first without much commentary and then discuss what I believe I learned from them afterwards.

EPISODES

In one early conversation, we discuss how aggressive Crash is. I define the word. Reynaldo seems taken by it; it may be one he hasn't known before. Reynaldo is a superb athlete and also has a temper. He gets into fights. He says with slow seriousness that he thinks managing anger is a hard thing—he understands how Crash feels when he takes his aggressive football behavior into other, less appropriate areas.

As we talk about Crash's family, Mohammad states that it is usually only men who work; no one replies, although it is not always true in the United States or even in the families of the other boys. I assume Mohammad is noticing that in Crash's family the mother works too. Mohammad's mother does not work outside the home.

In stark contrast to aggressive Crash, there is a character in the book named Penn who is a Quaker and a vegetarian, chooses to wear secondhand clothes, and believes in nonviolence. The boys are fascinated by what I tell them of Quakers. We discuss the idea of nonviolence and whether they themselves could be nonviolent. They don't really think so, and they certainly don't approve of wearing secondhand clothes as Penn does, but they are attracted to the character all the same, Lim especially. One day Lim writes on the blackboard as they arrive in my classroom, "If you are a Quaker, sign here." I believe I sort of stared, charmed.

A new girl joins the 8th grade and introduces herself to the math class at the request of the math teacher. She tells the class that she used to go to a Quaker school but has now transferred. Reynaldo and Lim report to me that they looked at each other and laughed, and no one else knew why. They came rushing to my office to tell me about it. A real live Quaker, they seem to be thinking—fiction and real life.

With Mohammad and his group on another day, I am defining the phrase "real estate" before we begin some silent reading. In the book Crash's mother works as a realtor, and I expect that the students won't know what this means. As I define the term for them, one of them tells me that there are other, better readers in the school. The others all nod. I explain to them that they each speak a language other than English at home and that that is why we have to do a lot of vocabulary work. They are amazed. They look at each other. They each appear not to have known that the others were not native English speakers and yet it never occurred to me that I needed to tell them this. We share a sentence or two in each native language. Later in the session, Mohammad stops the conversation to ask what "for lease" means—he has noticed it on signs as he walks around the neighborhood. There is a new ease in asking for vocabulary after we discover that I am the only one who speaks English as a first language.

The plot of the book leads us to talk of boyfriends and girlfriends, which then causes Mohammad to tell us that in his country marriages are often arranged, and the bride and groom are very young. Lim says, in his Cambodian community, this happens too. Mohammad says people say it is good to do it that way, for the boys especially, because then they don't get into flirting. Reynaldo and Carlos, from Brazil and the Dominican Republic respectively, look stunned and say nothing. Carlos has told us previously that he wants a car because his uncles have told him more girls will go out with him if he has a car. Again, the others listen silently. I suggest that a car might not be the best reason for someone to go out with Carlos, but I'm not sure anyone is hearing me.

There is a part in the book where Crash's beloved grandfather has a heart attack. Crash is so upset by this that he just throws some clothes on—no underwear, no socks, no jacket, just basic clothes—and runs out into the cold to buy his grandfather a Christmas present. He believes that if he buys his grandfather a Christmas present, he will survive. I was directing a conversation about the grandfather's illness when Mohammad, suddenly very serious, told me that he really didn't find this part realistic; in fact, he thinks it is outrageous because no 7th-grade boy would ever run out naked. I send the other kids off to read silently and ask Mohammad to find the passage where he gets the idea that Crash is naked. When we find it, I show him the phrase "he threw on his clothes." Oh, he says, I get it. I say, see, sometimes you read too fast. He says, no, the problem was not that; it was that it was figurative language. The expression "threw on his clothes" just hadn't worked for him. I don't know what he was imagining—throwing clothes out of his way? Throwing clothes, but not actually putting them on? I assume that it's just a case of an idiomatic phrase in English that he hadn't known but I remain a bit puzzled by his evident concern as we talk about this part. Later, in a different group, reading the same book, I notice that another child, a child who is a native speaker of English, has the same problem with this part of the book. He too is shocked and thinks Crash must be naked. What is up here? Both students were very concerned about Crash's situation, identifying strongly and yet misreading. I store this as something to wonder about even while I correct the mistake.

REFLECTION

At some point, I began to think again about the dying grandfather and the near nakedness of the frantic boy. First, I wondered if this scene was perhaps too emotional for many kids to read carefully since two of my students had misread it. I myself had never had a problem reading this part, but then I realized that I had found ridiculous the present Crash buys for his grandfather—in his anxiety, Crash runs to a secondhand store and buys the first thing he sees, a pair of red high heels. This book has a jokey middle school style in many places, and I had read this almost as a joke. Red high heels! How silly! What I began to see, thinking through the boys' reactions, was that I hadn't taken the situation seriously. We often say about struggling readers of these kinds of books, they miss the humor—but I see, here, that I missed the tragedy. They had not read correctly, true, but they had been upset by the grandfather's imminent death. From their difficulty, I began to see how powerful this scene is; this whole event, the illness of the beloved grandfather, is a huge emotional crisis for Crash. I had not fully experienced this scene, never taken it as seriously as it warranted, until the boys and their difficulty reading it brought it to my attention. In this case, documenting and then exploring my students' responses, in fact their misreading, opened me up to the book again and helped me see where my students live emotionally and how they allow literature to reach those places. Nor had they been overwhelmingly lost in the emotions; they had also each noticed that their reading did not really make sense—what teenage boy would run out in the street naked, as Mohammad asks. Both readers were monitoring their reading, even as they empathized with the situation—something all good readers do.

What about Lim and his continuing interest in Quakers? Lim is a Buddhist; later in the semester he tells us that when he was younger there was talk in his family of his becoming a monk. What does Lim, with his Buddhist background, know of nonviolence, of vegetarianism, both features of the character Penn? Maybe a lot. "If you're a Quaker, sign here," he writes. What was he thinking when he did that? What connections was he making between his life at home and the school where he now found himself? What concerns might his question contain?

Mohammad's statement about women and work—that it is usually men who work—is I think half statement, half question—he sort of puts it out there to see what will happen. The mother in the book works a great deal, perhaps too much as the book presents it, but eventually she cuts down on her work when her father, Crash's grandfather, gets ill. This Muslim child, whose mother dresses traditionally and who stays home, may be particularly aware of the difference in women's roles in this country and elsewhere. He is thinking about it; he may be making his statement to himself as much as to the rest of us. Similarly with the discussion about arranged marriage—the boys seem to be saying something to hear it, just putting it out there. Lim and Mohammad don't get much response from the other two when they comment on their knowledge of arranged marriage, and they don't seem to require it.

The students are bringing up, sometimes publicly, sometimes seemingly just for themselves, themes, values, important things that they are finding in the book:

Quakers and Buddhists
flirting
nonviolence and aggression
work and family
marriage

CONCLUSION

Teaching changed for me when I learned to take notes, to keep track of moments when my students surprised me, when they were especially serious or thoughtful or when they took the conversation in their own directions—and when they made surprising mistakes. Because I wrote these moments down, even roughly, they stayed in my mind. I was able to return to them, sometimes immediately, sometimes much later, sometimes with the students, sometimes alone in my mind, sometimes with others.

I told some of this story to a friend and fellow educator as we talked about democracy in education and she asked: But were the students changed by recognizing that they had different views on flirting, on arranged marriage, perhaps on women working or nonviolence?

Classroom community is often understood in very superficial ways or, rather, what it means is considered obvious. While what I have related may seem to be a series of small moments, the connections the students are making are, I believe, complex. They are recognizing themselves and recognizing other worlds around them, comparing, specifying, seeing what they hadn't seen before. What they are noticing matters to them. And I too realize that I am influenced by their feeling, their attention, their seriousness, and so we are occasionally silent.

Are these moments of cross-cultural understanding? Well, it shook some expectations. It surprised some of us, even shocked maybe; it provoked interest and curiosity, some feeling of disagreement maybe. My best metaphor for this moment, and there have been other moments like it, is fairly conventional, the expression *standing in another's shoes*—doing this, one might feel discomfort, surprise if one didn't step there on purpose, and the phrase is often also used to include empathy—feeling someone else's lousy shoes, different shoes, shoes that fit in one area and not another.

Whatever it was, I believe the experience deepened our community and enhanced our subsequent conversations.

Part III

CHILDREN WITH SPECIAL NEEDS

CHAPTER 7

Jillian

Appearing and Disappearing

INTRODUCTION

The following two accounts, in this chapter and Chapter 8, explore another aspect of the rewards that result from stopping time and reflecting on student work and words. These two chapters are accounts of my work with two students, Jillian and Jessica, who had mental health diagnoses; this label and the behavior that it described made it difficult at first for me to see them clearly, and to connect with them.

Dirck Roosevelt, a longtime practitioner and mentor in the work of what he terms "teaching as a form of attention," states, "observation is a way one actually comes to truly like a student" (Roosevelt, 1998). I believe this statement is true—as one observes and puts words to paper to describe the student and their activity, one comes to care. And reciprocally, as the student senses the close attention, they may in response gain courage and reveal themselves more and more. Paying close attention to another makes the relationship. Writing careful observations whenever possible strengthens the liking as well. I believe that was the case in these two final stories.

I will begin with Jillian. It is important in this story to recognize that the events took place in a school where teachers regularly talked to each other and shared observations in both formal and informal ways; it reminds me of the deep rewards of teaching when conversations about students are a part of the fabric of the day. It is also an incomplete story, full of starts and stops. Jillian was a difficult child, a child in the mental health system as I've said. I never figured out an overall effective way to teach her on a day-to-day basis, nor can I claim that, when I last saw her, she was out of trouble. She was a noisy child, someone who shouted at teachers and at other students. She was emotional and angry. Sometimes she was physically aggressive. Once angry, she was very difficult to deal with. At other times, she could be calm and participate successfully. One never knew. She frightened the other students. What remains most important to me about teaching this child were the occasional moments when I was stopped in my tracks by the sudden clarity and the intensity of what she did or said. These moments presented a view of her beyond her difficulties.

READING GROUP—4TH GRADE

My reading groups are usually filled with children who are having difficulty reading, but they may also be formed around particular children whose social problems suggest a group might be helpful. Jillian's story was a typically complicated example. She was below grade level in reading achievement, but not far below. In 3rd and 4th grades, she was reluctant to read independently at all. In fact, she appeared not to be able to sit quietly for any length of time. When she did read, her teacher pointed out that she read very slowly, surprisingly so. Of most concern, she was socially isolated and frequently very angry and aggressive.

Her teacher and I arranged a reading group for Jillian when she was in 4th grade. Her teacher had suggested putting her in with girls at or above grade level as a message to her about her true potential. Her teacher felt that her emotional health problems were very serious—she felt that at times Jillian was out of touch with reality—but that she was basically competent academically. This group read *Because of Winn-Dixie* by Kate DiCamillo and Jillian kept up, although with some difficulty. Still, her slow rate did increase noticeably. Since she was a very volatile personality, however, she was often absent or in the office for wild behaviors, like throwing things in the classroom or uncontrollable tantrums. There was one day when I could not get her to come out from under the table. The group did not really gel for her—she had initially asked me what she was doing with this group of girls; they were all engaged readers and in general well-behaved children and she evidently felt her difference. Nevertheless, she did appear to enjoy the book; she engaged irregularly, but often well, with it. But she did not seem comfortable. She was there, participating, and then she wasn't. Looking back, I suspect that her teacher and I should have been checking in more regularly. To be in this group was a challenge for Jillian, and we should have been more attentive to that.

READING GROUP—6TH GRADE

It is the custom in my school to stay with the same teacher for two years. Jillian moved on to a new teacher for 5th and 6th grades. In 5th grade, her teacher did not suggest that she be in a reading group at all. At that point, her teacher did not feel Jillian could get along socially in a group. She was too often defiant in class and did not regularly participate in her schoolwork. She was frequently late to school and in many incidents was described by her teacher as "wild-eyed" and out of control.

Late in the Fall of her 6th-grade year, this same teacher told me she felt Jillian was now becoming a reader. She was reading a lot, not always when she was supposed to, but reading all the same. The teacher felt she had grown in some ways and was more comfortable with her fellow students and was ready to read with at least one other child. The following narrative is based on notes I took as we read together. I include references to conversations with her classroom teacher as well. Both her classroom teacher and I were struck by the times when Jillian participated appropriately in school; these may appear to be very small events at times, but, since she was otherwise often sullen, angry, or just quiet, when she appeared engaged, it was memorable. Sharing these moments with each other helped us see Jillian as more than just a problem.

Jillian had just devoured *Money Hungry*, a book by Sharon Flake, which is told in the first person by a young Black female protagonist. Jillian, as a young African American female, had identified strongly, and since there is another book by the same author, *The Skin I'm In*, she wanted to read that next.

There was another child whose schedule meshed and who needed a boost in her reading. Sarah, unlike Jillian, was the kind of child we think of as easy to teach. She was diligent, reserved, quietly-mannered. She could be opinionated and 6th-grade-stubborn, but she generally did as she was asked. By this time, Jillian, although she was outspoken, often rude, and demanded a lot of attention, had developed a sort of ironic smile, as if, at least some of the time, she knew she was being outrageous and thought it was kind of funny. They both had an eagerness about them, and a sense of humor. I enjoyed them, and they seemed to be comfortable with each other, so a group was formed. Looking back, I would say that it was wise to make the group only two children. Perhaps the 4th-grade group had been too large, and the other students were already friendly with one another; it may have been awkward for Jillian, although we didn't realize it at the time. Sarah was quiet and at ease; she participated but not in an assertive manner. The two children liked the comfy chairs I provided my reading groups and seemed to find it a relaxing spot.

We began with The *Skin I'm In.*

I normally opened the group sessions with a routine. Often I would preview vocabulary I thought necessary. These were generally what we call "tier 2" words, ones that were not entirely unfamiliar but could use some clarification. I would introduce one or two of these words and give the meaning, and then we would explore together what we knew of them (cf. Beck et al., 2002). These conversations always followed the same format. It was easy for the students to participate, offering their own examples of, for example, a "dwelling" or of "defiance" after I had given the initial definition, and I think Jillian enjoyed them. Often, when the word then appeared in the book, there would be some excitement, as if they hadn't been convinced that it would.

Jillian liked reading out loud; she often requested it. And so, after the vocabulary and any introductory work, we would read out loud at the start of each group meeting. She seemed to go faster when she read out loud. Perhaps it was more enveloping to hear the words and in that way this method supported her attention. Still, I valued silent reading, and so after a page or two, we would move on to silent reading and then, after 15 minutes or so, we would discuss what we had read.

I often set up a question to read with, and when I did, we would sometimes write to each other in our notebooks, offering opinions and observations on the question as we read. Jillian wrote fairly fluently, and this was something she enjoyed. I think it felt like a private conversation to her.

In all of the routines, Jillian seemed comfortable and was able to participate. In contrast, once it became time to discuss our reading together, she often became awkward. When I asked for an interpretation or an emotional response, she usually said "I don't know." I wondered what to make of this. Was she intimidated by Sarah's greater facility? Or my questions? They were intended to be very open-ended. Could she really not make her responses public?

The following notes and narrative pieces recount moments when Jillian became suddenly more responsive, or when I felt her presence strongly. I sometimes call these "struck-bys," moments when I was struck.

EARLY STRUCK-BYS

Sarah was talking about why writing in a diary may have helped the main character, Maleeka, to cope. "She had a sort of different world in there," she tells me. Jillian, however, says, "I don't know," when I ask her if she agrees. Finally, Jillian does say that she would not have liked to have Miss Saunders, a character with burn scars on her face, as a teacher. When I ask why, Jillian says she doesn't know. Finally, looking down, she mutters, "It would be weird to look at that face." This was a very personal response for Jillian. It felt visceral. I was struck. And I was reminded of Darius (see Chapter 2).

Halfway through the book Sarah had to go to Trinidad for a family wedding. She was gone for three weeks. While Sarah was gone, at Jillian's request, she and I read a Walter Dean Meyers book, *Scorpions*. She wanted to continue to read about Black characters, she told me, and so she chose this book. *Scorpions* is pretty gritty, about gangs and violence and families with little way out.

In the beginning of the book the mother is returning very late to her apartment where her younger son and daughter are waiting. I knew that she has been visiting her older son who has been shot; I assumed she had been to a hospital to see him. Jillian, however, realized that the visiting hours described were not for a hospital, but a prison; she knew this, she told me, because she has visited her dad in prison and "I know how it goes there." She didn't ask me to respond. Again she seemed calm and present.

I hadn't been sure that I wanted to read this book, but somehow her knowing things I didn't and explaining to me about her father in the way she did convinced me.

Next, I see in my notes that Jillian missed a week of school. Then she was in and out of the office for her behavior. She finished the book without me. We tried to have a conversation about it, but it was unsuccessful.

LATER IN THE WINTER

In early February, Jillian began to come again somewhat consistently to read with me, although usually by herself and not always on schedule. I wrote that she was showing some ability to calm her behavior down once there. The following are notes from that period.

Feb. Note

Jillian came into my room and just read silently while I taught some other kids. She still goes very slowly when reading silently; she goes much faster when reading out loud. An unusual pattern.

Feb. Note

Jillian pops in with a book. She says she has permission to join me. I am teaching apostrophe review with some 4th-graders. She joins in, is very nice to the younger kids, asking their names and helping with the apostrophes. Then her teacher walks in—it turns out Jillian didn't have permission to be there. But the teacher, seeing her engagement, leaves her be.

After the apostrophe work is over, I send her to make things right with her teacher. As she leaves, she says, mostly to herself, "I *was* mad at her." I felt that I was overhearing an unusual, private moment of reflection.

I wrote to her teacher:

> I think her relationship with you is really helping her mature. The other day when you found her getting apostrophe practice without permission (I should have known it wasn't pure love for apostrophes that kept her there), she looked at the floor after you left and said to herself, I *was* mad at her. It seemed like she was saying that she realized you had treated her well by letting her stay, and she wasn't mad anymore, and so she now began to question the previous events. There was a lot more self-reflection in her expression than I usually see, I thought.

Later in February we decide to try again to form a group. This time in addition to Sarah and Jillian we include Lea, who also has a lot of trouble reading and paying attention. I had been trying to give the choice of the book to the students, but we have not been successful at choosing a book.

Note

> Jillian got very excited. She had asked if the group could read out loud, and then she was sort of playing teacher, instructing the others as to their turns. It was funny and not rude, but a little out there. Sometimes I think she needs this sort of space, sometimes I'm not so sure. I walked her back to the classroom because I was hoping I could help her settle down. She was quite able to talk about the necessity of settling down, but not so successful at doing it. I stuck my head in the classroom to alert her teacher.

I typically walked Jillian back to class each day, and because her regular classroom was just down the hall, I often had a chance to share thoughts with her classroom teacher.

Note

Discarded another book. I will choose the book rather than let the students try. It doesn't seem to be working

Notes on Reading *Stargirl*

> I chose *Stargirl* by Jerry Spinelli. The following notes and reflections give the feeling of reading *Stargirl* with Jillian that Spring. Again, they detail sporadic

attendance and small moments of what I interpreted as engagement. I would be pleased and then disappointed.

March 10 Note

After a few false starts, we began *Stargirl*, the story of a very unconventional middle-school girl. After beginning the book, the girls all notice how Stargirl doesn't care what people think. We talk about what this means. Sarah says her mother says that she must care—it is important to the family. Jillian says her sister doesn't care—her evidence is that her sister doesn't bother to match her clothes.

March 15 Note

Teacher reports to me that Jillian asked where Kossovo is. And then, with concentration she worked on the map to find it. Her teacher is struck by her focus. Kossovo is in the news at this time as the scene of fighting and even massacres. Is she stuck by this violence? By the news?

March 20 Note

It's been hard to get Jillian going with *Stargirl*. She asks at one point for another book by a Black author, although at another time she has told me it doesn't matter. Then she loses the book for a day or two.

April 1 Note

I receive a report from her teacher that Jillian had to be sent to the office for her wild behavior, and that when she returned, she delivered a bizarre chanting series of apologies. We lost another day.

April 4 Note

From her teacher I learn that Jillian arrived at school at 12:30. When she came to me, she was noisy and hard to settle. We read, but it took work to keep her focused. However, when she wrote a journal entry about *Stargirl*, it was clear and showed engagement.

She mentioned how her teacher was now using *Scorpions* for a reading group, and that she had already read *Scorpions,* and also that she had finished the book ahead of me. She seemed to want some praise or feel her influence on the teacher's choice. This was not something I usually noticed in her. She doesn't usually seem to care. A change?

April 17 Note

Jillian is kicked out of participating in her class play.

April 20 Note

Jillian not present because she has lost *Stargirl.*

April 23 Note

Jillian comes in with Sarah. I have trouble getting Jillian to focus. She writes words she wants me to define for her but isn't focusing deeply on the plot. Sarah tells us that Stargirl is "blind." She says that Stargirl gets into situations in a blind way. Should Stargirl have gone to the funeral when she might not have known the person who died? Sarah asks. Jillian thinks she may have known him actually. This is clearly not the case in the text. What was Jillian thinking? Was the funeral upsetting or had she misread?

Notebook Dialogue

April 27 Note

We read silently. The narrator of the book has become infatuated with Stargirl and follows her on a long walk into the desert. Jillian and I correspond about this in her notebook.

Me: Why is Stargirl walking so far?
Jillian: I don't know the book doesn't tell me. Because she probably wants to go out because it was a hard day at school or something
Me: Why is he following her?
Jillian: Because he wants to know if she's real and he didn't stay because his parents would probably wonder.

My Reflection on Dialogue: In the first part of this exchange Jillian begins by refusing to answer in a way that was very common for her. Then she crosses this out and makes a guess. Stargirl does have hard days at school, but there is little evidence in the book that she is bothered by this, or that she specifically had such a day before this long walk. Jillian, of course, does have hard days, often. This feels to me like a big moment—she is using her experience to suggest something Stargirl might be feeling.

In the second exchange, the boy, who is the narrator, does suggest in the text that his parents might wonder where he is. Jillian adds the idea that he wants to know if Stargirl is real. This is a very pertinent idea—Stargirl is part real middle schooler and part sort of mythic creature. I use this idea of Jillian's in subsequent group discussions.

Dinosaur Episode

April 1

Jillian pops in, having found the book after losing it for a few days. She says it is getting better like I told her it would. She proceeds to give me a complete summary. I don't ask for this. I'm just checking in, but Jillian seems to feel that it's what she ought to do, so she stops me from dismissing her so she can complete her summary. During the summary, Jillian stands tall and still, making full eye contact.

Because there is a paleontologist in the next chapter, I make sure to explain before she leaves the meaning of the word to prepare her for her at home reading. We start talking about dinosaurs. She tells me she held dinosaur poop in her hand once. She continues to stand tall and reasonably still; looking at me, she puts her hands together and enacts holding and touching the dinosaur poop. I tell her about uncovering dinosaur prints when I was on a geology class field trip on the banks of the Connecticut River. She asks how the prints were formed and why the river has changed since that time.

My Reflection: She never asks me questions of this kind. She seems fascinated by the eons of time represented by the bones, the poop she touched, and the dinosaur footprints I saw. She was amazingly calm in her body and focused in her mind. I felt a difference.

Paleontologist Episode

April 30

I have posted a sentence for the group about Archie, the paleontologist in the book. I ask the kids to explain it. Lea is working on remembering what happened with Archie. Sarah is not there. Jillian sets out to explain to Lea about Archie and the kind of relationship he has with the kids in the book: "the house is more like a museum, only you can touch things. But it might be a bit creepy, full of bones. But Archie seems really nice." She says that he loves bones, and that kids might like him. She goes on to explain to Lea how, because Stargirl is weird, she might hang around with Archie since he is also unusual.

My Reflection: This conversation is singular. I connect it to our earlier conversation about the bones and her evident interest in dinosaurs. She seems to relate to Archie's collecting and his interest in the remote past, and she is explaining him to another child in very pleasant, connected ways. She is unusually aware of her audience and what they need to know. Again, as she speaks, she is noticeably calm—her body and voice are in control—she is focused. And she seems to have a very nice feeling for the character, Archie, some genuine liking.

I share her comments with her full teaching team. They were all impressed.

CONCLUSION

As I look back, I noticed some of the moments that struck me may have some connection one to another. Kosovo, the place she needed to find on the map in 6th grade, was the scene of a lot of violence at the time. Her telling me about the way things are in jails and then her response to the burnt face of the teacher in *The Skin I'm In* were all perhaps also scenes of high emotion and sorrow. And then, on a different tack, her denial at first that she was unconventional (although she admits her sister was) reminds me, as she describes Archie, that she now seems to have quite an appreciation for his unusualness—as she tells the other students, Stargirl was weird and so was Archie the paleontologist, so they probably got along. Her preference for reading outloud now seems to me to be a way to engage her whole body, voice, ears, lungs—perhaps this helps her settle down or to focus. I will use this idea with other children.

Did I see clearly that there might be themes in her comments at the time? No, I did not. Perhaps it would have helped if I had. I don't know. I know that when she spoke with seriousness, she calmed her body. And at those times I did give her space, and I did think about what she said even if I wasn't always able to connect immediately across other remarks. And this is often the way it is—one is struck, but fuller interpretation may come later. But the child has made use of the space.

This is of course an incomplete account. She would lose the book, be in the office, be hard to settle down, and, because of the confusion, my notes would occasionally become sporadic. My enduring picture is of Jillian standing before me, tall and focused, enacting how she held the dinosaur poop, and then asking me to explain further about the dinosaur footprints I saw by the Connecticut River. She was an anxious child, and an unpredictable, often loud, often contentious child. And yet I have observed these moments when her body was still, and she spoke, seemingly, what was on her mind. As teachers our moral commitment is to believe that this child too has ideas and to listen when she expresses them. While over time she seemed to appear and to disappear, when she was interested, she seemed to grow in maturity almost perceptibly. Never have I seen the literature on teaching children with these kinds of problems address the importance of the child's interests (see National Education Association, 2023) and yet I think it truly is something important. In both Jillian's case and in the following chapter when they were deeply interested, they were in a different kind of control of themselves.

What we were able to see of Jillian was the result of a sustained interest in and hope for her by her teachers who sought and responded to her best moments as well as to her problems.

CHAPTER 8

Finding an Interest

To continue with the idea of interests in children with mental health diagnoses, I present here Jessica. I was working one-on-one with Jessica who was 11 years old. She was in a classroom for students regarded as being high-functioning autistics. Jessica rarely spoke at all, and when she did, she was hard to understand and spoke in short, gutural bursts, using few words at a time. She made only fleeting eye contact. Teachers communicated by matching words with arms: Did she want an orange (teacher raises left arm) or an apple (teacher raises right arm)? Jessica would then point at one arm or the other. She did very little schoolwork. When I first watched Jessica in school the main thing she did was pound her head with her hand and pick up teeny things (perhaps actually there, I was never sure) from her desk and from her shirt. She did this constantly. Some of the specialists who saw Jessica one-on-one thought she was understanding more than was apparent. Others did not agree; they regarded her as having low intelligence and considered moving her to a different classroom more suited to children who couldn't learn easily. It was difficult to know. However, it was true that she had learned to read and write and had acquired basic math skills, and she had talked some in her earlier schooling. Still, when I met her she was so preoccupied with her head smacks that I thought she could hardly hear or attend to those around her.

AT FIRST

I was tapped to provide about 12 hours a week of additional language support for Jessica. My strategy in these situations has always been to find something the student is interested in, a place for me to make contact with the real living child engaged with the world, and so I set out to determine what we were to talk about. But how was I to identify the interests of a child like this, a child who engaged so minimally with the world around her? It did not appear that she had any interests.

Observation

I soon witnessed that at recess she would spend all her time digging for worms. She would put on plastic surgical gloves and then squat in the school garden, raking through the dirt with her gloved fingers, picking out tiny worms and other insects and dropping them on the sidewalk. She would do this by herself, and often would have a tantrum when it was time to return inside. And yet, what could I learn from this? She didn't like to touch the worms, she did like raking through the dirt, she didn't like to stop. It wasn't much of a start, although these features did fit with what I knew of autism. I had taught many children with this diagnosis who demonstrated tactile sensitivity, a tendency to perseverate, and rigidity in following schedules and routines.

I turned to two masters of observation. Patricia Carini directs us to include in our observations physical details, observations of stance, movement, and appearance (Himley, 2002). This was an area I had paid less attention to in the past, preferring to focus on language. Clifford Geertz, the anthropologist, suggests that an aid to interpreting one's observations is to find a metaphor, something that the observer is reminded of in the event or the person, and then to make comparisons (Geertz, 1984).

Jessica, as she looked for worms, made me think of a small, taut bird, wings folded in, her head bent forward and tight. As she explored the dirt in front of her, she squatted all the way down, her bum just off the ground, and she remained apparently comfortable in this position for 10 or 15 minutes. She appeared oblivious to all else around her. She was able to find almost invisible worms—her vision was sharp. She successfully kept her clothes immaculate. I saw her intentness, her focus, her balance, and her tension.

Reflection

I could see that she was focused and intent, but I wondered, was it part of being interested? Maybe. On the other hand, it also seemed possible that this activity might provide some physical comfort to this very tense child, or some stimulation that she craved. I wondered if raking the dirt was satisfying a physical need that she had, providing some stimulation that she craved and thus actually keeping her from much awareness of the outside word. I really didn't know. Which was it? Or could both be true?

MY FIRST MOVES

I decided to join in. I would talk a bit as we raked the earth, but she would not, other than to answer simple questions sometimes, with very tight, abbreviated nods of her head, looking away from me. When I suggested something about being gentle with the worms, or when I wondered aloud about their behavior, for example whether they might be cold where she left them exposed on the sidewalk, she wouldn't respond or indicate that she'd heard.

I began the practice of counting down the remaining seconds for her when outside time was ending, intoning the numbers slowly and rhythmically. She stopped raking and got ready to go in without a tantrum. Did she need this rhythmic counting to transition calmly? Did the rhythm of the count help her emerge from her all-encompassing search for worms and return to the reality of school?

When I worked with her in the school, we would go over some of her upcoming classwork together. I used pictures and drawings to give her some exposure ahead of class to the vocabulary and ideas that the teacher was planning to address. Sometimes, as we walked into class after our session, I was able to let the teacher know what Jessica had practiced, and the teacher would ask her a relevant question during class discussion. Jessica was sometimes able, and willing, to answer, briefly but out loud, in class. This was new. We teachers relished these moments, and Jessica received a lot of praise. It was apparent that she was able to learn and to respond. But what she thought or felt we did not know. She gave no indication.

STUDYING WORMS

I decided to pursue the worms. They were my only clue. I purchased a worm bin and some red worms, and I kept them in my office. After we had done our classwork, we would turn to the worms. We picked them up, felt them—Jessica with plastic gloves on. When I asked her to, Jessica would read about them in articles I had found. She always read silently; or I think she read—she would go awfully fast, so I did wonder whether she was actually reading. The time she spent reading had a quality of stiffness and tension, certainly not relaxation. After she finished, we would write back and forth in my notebook. This turned out to be a form of documentation that was invaluable later when I wanted to look back to see exactly what she had "said" as I taught her. What I saw was that I would ask her questions about the reading, but the questions were my questions, what I wanted her to know, not what she thought or wondered. Sometimes what she wrote in her answers to my queries appeared to be guesses. She didn't volunteer any questions, observations, or ideas. When I asked her to draw the worms, she would but the result was sloppy and rapidly done. No sign of looking closely, of real interest!

She looked at me now and came with me willingly. She rapped her head much less when she was working with me. Her teaching team thought she was making progress, but I still didn't know what she might be thinking about worms. I must admit that I wondered if she was thinking at all.

The Worm–Apple Study

After a few weeks I decided to begin an investigation with the worms. I added an apple to the worm bin, and I wondered aloud if the worms would eat it. Jessica nodded, indicating that she thought so. She also nodded when I asked if she would share this question with her class. We brought the worm bin into the classroom and asked each student to make two predictions: would the worms eat the apple and if so, how long would it take? At her desk, Jessica filled out a chart I gave her, noting the guesses of each of her classmates. She sat up straight, she recorded each of her classmates' guesses, and she corrected my spelling of one child's name. She did not rap her head! She did not look for tiny specks on her shirt or desk!

After a week had passed, Jessica and I checked on the worm bin and we saw that the apple was indeed being eaten. We decided to rejoin the class and show them. I took Jessica up front with me, and we showed everyone the worms and the apple. The bin was also full of worm castings, worm poop, which looked just like dirt. Students made a variety of comments about decomposition and the worms eating the apple and they also suggested that there was dirt in the worm bin. Jessica told the kids out loud "no dirt," and then she explained, "worms poop." Again, no head rapping; she was up in front of the class in an easy stance.

Her teachers were all excited. We had not known that she would be comfortable in front of the class or that she would speak in response to the others. She seemed focused, her body calm. Everyone noticed her body and mentioned how present and calm she was.

A first step had been made. I was delighted. Where to go next? While something wonderful happened with the apple investigation, I remained uncomfortable with how Jessica was functioning, and also with how I was teaching. I wrote in my notes my distress that "she won't help me feed the worms"; I regularly brought in food scraps and when I suggested that she take a turn putting them into the bin, she always refused. She seemed rough with the worms, perhaps not deliberately so, but very offhand. And she still did not ask any questions about them or respond to the questions I asked—I would sit beside her, modeling my wondering—were the worms cold? Did they like the sun?—but she would ignore me, as far as I could tell from her behavior.

Reflection

What is an interest anyway? How do we recognize one? What are the features of an interest? I decided to think about my experience with other children and their interests. I realized that I expected that Jess, like the others, would participate in my wonder, and would also begin to ask her own questions. I thought that she would notice things on her own; interested children often notice things that I have missed entirely, something I enjoy a great deal. And I hoped that she would care, that she would develop the connections that I had seen other children develop with the things that interested them. In my experience these qualities—being curious, highly observant of details, and in some sort of affective relationship with the phenomenon—were usually part of being interested, and Jessica was not showing me any of this. Interest is a sort of energy, in my experience, an energy which connects you and the student with the object of interest. She may have been making progress, but I didn't feel like we were in this together.

Peer Pressure

A question arose from the other students: Would the seeds from the apple grow in the poop? Leading to a follow-up question from the class: Will seeds grow better in the poop or in plain dirt? Jessica predicted dirt. When I asked her why, she wrote, "poop is dirty." Other kids predicted poop; they said there might be nutrients in it which would help growth.

I wondered at the time, and later, Did Jessica care about this question or was she just going through the motions? It did seem like a real answer, though. The following day she changed her mind to agree with the class consensus that seeds would grow better in poop. At first I thought she was bowing to peer pressure. I laughed; I thought it was delightful and something new—she had certainly seemed oblivious to peer pressure before. However, I did not see this development as particularly important in terms of engaging with the topic.

Reflection

Later, I saw this episode differently. Now, while Jessica certainly adopted the majority position, I see it not in the negative light suggested by "bowing to peer pressure," but as a positive engagement with her peers' ideas. Whether she was actually thinking through the other children's statements I do not know, but changing her prediction demonstrated engagement with the group in a way I had not seen before. And perhaps it really was an intellectual move as well, a step away from the immediate and visceral response, "poop, yuck," to some consideration of what poop might in fact do for apple seeds. Here again I would say that having my notes was crucial. This event might have passed me by, but having written a slight reference to what had happened kept it in my mind for further reflection. And of course, I do not finally know why she changed her answer, but wondering about it, even without a final answer, meant that I was imagining a more complex intellectual life for her—I was seeing more possibilities and my expectations for her grew.

We decided to leave the worm bin in the classroom rather than my office. Jessica negotiated a deal with her classroom teachers that if she finished her classwork, she could spend time with the classroom worms. During these explorations, she found a worm egg (which is very hard to do, as they are tiny); she noticed a worm that seemed about to lay eggs; she noticed one pooping. She shared each of these sightings with the other students, who would crowd excitedly around her. Jessica was finding a unique place in the class. She was interacting with and paying more attention to the other students. Even in the cluster of bodies, she acted reasonably comfortable.

But still she asked no questions. Or so it seemed.

I contacted a friend, Dirck Roosevelt. He is now a professor, but also a former teacher deeply schooled in the work of Patricia Carini. He loves to think about kids. After describing Jessica, I asked him: Is it possible to be interested without asking a question? He pondered and then said, "Jessica may be questioning with her fingers." Hmmm. This picture of asking question with her fingers stayed in my mind.

THREE MORE PUZZLING MOMENTS

After our success with the worm–apple experiment, the teaching team suggested a few other opportunities for Jessica to get up in front of the class to present her work. As I have said, I try to note those moments when I am surprised or even distressed by what happened, so that I can reflect later on my response and on what my students did and what they might have been thinking. As the semester went on, more puzzling events led to my growing understanding of Jessica and also of the ways in which we were sometimes at cross-purposes.

What Is Appropriate Intervention?

Jessica's science class was studying pollution, and so I gave her an essay I had simplified for her to read about how worms clean the soil. When I began with a simple comprehension question about the article, she answered "shark"; this was a reference to something written above the article, on the same page, but not what I had, clearly I thought, asked her to read. Not a good beginning to my plan! Was she understanding me at all? Momentarily, we seemed back at square one.

I reoriented and we went on. As we did, she seemed to be nervously pointing to spots where she thought the answer was to my questions, looking at me for support. Did she read what I gave her? Was she derailed by some terrible anxiety to be right? Was the article too difficult?

In some disappointment, I continued with the article, now explaining more, asking new questions, and acting out a good deal of the content as we went through it. Finally, we wrote back and forth what you see below.

CB: What dangerous things do worms eat?
Jessica: Heavy metal.
CB: Are there dangerous things in the worm's poop?
Jessica: No.
CB: How can we make our soil cleaner?
Jessica: Worm poop helps the earth clean.
CB: If there is a lot of pollution and the soil gets dirty and full of dangerous things, how can worms help?
Jessica: The worms keep the dirty stuff inside they clean the earth.

The final sentence contains the point of the article—that worms can keep heavy metals inside their body, thus cleaning the soil. In the final sentence she used "earth" which I did not use, and her use of the word "stuff" again felt like her own word—this made me think that this was her own thinking, that she was not parroting what I had said. The last sentence was the longest sentence she had written to me to date. And I remember also that she appeared by then much less anxious, taking turns writing with me, looking at my responses before going on.

But to get there I had done a lot of acting out and continuing to question her. My repeated questioning resembled what I call "pulling teeth," where teachers keep at their student until they get the answer they want. I dislike and disapprove of this style of interaction. I prefer to ask my students open-ended questions and then sit back and let them explain themselves. I began to see that my practice with Jessica was different than usual, much more one-sided. I attempted to change my pattern, to wait longer for her to respond, but I was not very successful. I would very quickly begin to worry, to feel that she needed help, or just that she was wrong, and then I couldn't stop myself from providing hints in the form of further questions, physical enactment, and more information.

Reflection

However, much later, as I again reviewed these interactions in my mind, and questioned my inability to change them very much, I for the first time wondered if Jessica felt that this was a problem. I have always imagined that students did not enjoy feeling interrogated, or being questioned repeatedly until the teacher receives the desired answer, and that for them to think on their own, I had to be quiet and wait. But did *Jessica* feel this way? Did she feel that I was poking at her, correcting her, interrupting her thinking? There was one time when I became annoyed with her as she seemed to be guessing at a parts of speech exercise sheet her English teacher had given her. I said a bit abruptly and with some irritation, "But those aren't nouns," pointing at what she had indicated. She looked up at me and just waited. I defined the parts of speech for her, and then she easily and comfortably, it seemed to me, returned to the sheet and corrected her answers.

As the year continued, I realized that this was not unusual. She often waited for me to respond after she wrote something, willingly refining her answer after each of my turns as she did in our development of the worms' role in cleaning the dirt. Was she perhaps using my questions as some sort of scaffold to express herself? Maybe, although I was doing something that I did not generally believe in, I was in fact helping her put her thoughts into language and perhaps helping her to process my words as well. Truly, she was not practiced in putting her thoughts out there. From this time on, I tried to remain open to the idea that my impulse to give Jessica more information, to keep on her, was not always wrong. I tried to stay attentive to how she was responding and to what my feelings and intuitions were in turn.

Taking Initiative

In the case above, I did want her to understand the article's point; however, I also remained committed to the idea that she should express her own ideas. I still wasn't hearing any of her thinking or her feelings. I modeled the kind of "thinking out loud" that I appreciated, but she, unlike other students in my experience, remained silent. To me, once again, it appeared that if she wasn't taking any initiative, she wasn't fully engaged, even though she was more relaxed and seemed to be learning. However, in these two following puzzling moments, my documentation helped me to see that she had taken more initiative than I recognized at my first look.

Worms Communicate

The first one occurred when Jessica was presenting in front of her class. She and I had read an article about communication among worms. The article claimed that when worms cluster together, they often then head out in the same direction, and that this indicates that they have somehow made a group decision, and thus that they are able to communicate. We had seen worms do this clustering. Once we were up in front of the class, though, and I asked her to tell the class what we had learned about what happens when worms cluster together, she told the class that they do it because they are cold. This was true, but it was old information for us—we read it a while ago, and it was not the reason presented in the article we had just read. I was distressed, afraid she had missed the point of our reading. Later, when I reminded her of what we had read, she drew a picture of a cluster, and then of a couple of worms going off together, indicating, as the article had, that they have communicated and made a shared plan. She looked at me as if to say, "See. I do understand that worms communicate." But that is not what she had told her class. What's up here? I asked in my field notes.

Convection

In this next example, Jessica and I had prepared to present ideas of convection to the class at her science teacher's suggestion—the teacher had asked her to do this because she felt Jessica understood convection well.

We practiced demonstrating the interaction of hot (red food coloring) and cold (blue food coloring) water in an aquarium. She agreed to explain to the kids that hot water rises. When we presented, she was focused and organized. The kids were thrilled to watch the demonstration and to feel the different temperatures of the water. But when I asked Jessica to explain what was happening as the hot red water visibly rose above the cold blue, she said, "Lava." I laughed and remonstrated, asking very specifically, "What is the hot water doing?" She said, somewhat stiffly, "It's rising." She was asked to draw a diagram of what had happened, and she did it very well, with hot water rising, cool water sinking. Later I wrote to her, asking why she had said "lava" and she wrote, "it's red." Then she included a small drawing of lava spreading above what was evidently an erupting volcano.

Reflection

In thinking over these last two puzzling presentations, my first realization was that I had an expected format for these presentations that we did together: I would ask the initial question and Jessica was supposed to answer as we had practiced. I was invested in this—I wanted her to look smart. (She had not always looked smart in her school career.) But she didn't always comply. And then I would feel that we had failed.

Upon reflection, it seems in the case of the cold worms that she was almost feeling the worms being cold, huddling and then warming up; a very visceral idea that we had acted out earlier. She perhaps liked the idea of worms huddling in comfort and made that feeling the focus of what she wanted to tell the other students, rather than the idea that they communicate.

As to her response in the convection demonstration: I knew she was fascinated by volcanoes. She had been studying the culture of Hawaii, and in science she had been looking at the ring of fire, at volcanoes and tectonic plates. She asked me one day, "How was Hawaii made?" and explained to me that she meant, How did the islands form? This was the very first question I ever heard from her, and it was about the role of volcanoes in the formation of the island chain. The hot water in our aquarium, as it rose and spread out, did indeed resemble an eruption of lava. I now believe she was putting together her interest in volcanoes and the demonstration of convection currents.

My point in these examples is that I now see Jessica as having chosen what she wanted to say, making comments and presenting connections and ideas that she wanted to offer to her fellow students. She was taking some initiative but I did not initially see it this way—as I said, when she strayed from our plan, I found it both puzzling and unclear. In the case of the lava especially she did not verbalize the connection she was making between convection currents and volcanoes. Without that connection expressed verbally, I think my worry that she hadn't understood made it difficult for me to relax and listen. I was now the one who was tense.

Because we interacted regularly through writing in my notebook, I was able to look back over her answers to my questions. Without this opportunity, I am not sure I would have realized what she was thinking about. This realization again changed how I heard her and made it easier for me to give her time to respond. Now I usually remembered to come back to ask what she meant when I failed to understand her.

SPRING

By spring, her advisor told me Jessica was now using her voice in every class. She answered questions. She talked to the kids at lunch, and the other kids talked to her. She never hit her head anymore, or picked at her T-shirt. She made eye contact a good deal of the time. That she was intelligent had become clear.

Still, I continued to worry that she was rough with the worms, which we continued to tend together, or at least quite offhand. One day, as we were poking some worms in my office, we were able to determine which end was the front by watching how they escaped from the poking. She was excited to report on this discovery and so we rejoined the class and again set up in the front of the room. She demonstrated, the kids were fascinated; they came up to the front to see. Then, during the poking demonstration, one big worm started to bleed. We stopped and returned it to the worm bin. I felt responsible since I had given Jessica a rough implement for her poking, rather than the soft spoon we had used earlier, which I could not find. I didn't say so, but I was kicking myself for being careless.

Two days later, Jessica brought me the same worm and showed me where it had healed. She was answering the worry of a few days earlier. Was it her worry? Had she felt mine? Or both? In any case, a true case of empathy.

There is much more to say about her worm studies and the turtles that we subsequently studied. But let me end by pointing to another aspect of her life in school. My notes remind me that by Spring, she was getting angry often. She would stomp her feet; she broke materials a few times when teachers didn't give her what she wanted. At the same time, though, she began truly caring for the worms, for example, breaking open an apple with her bare hands to make it easier for them to eat, an idea all her own. And finally, she began giving me worms to carry when she found them outdoors. When she did this, it felt ceremonial. I received a tremendously strong vibe of kindness; she moved me almost to tears.

When I was preparing to leave my position at the school, since Jessica no longer needed me so badly, I arranged for us to have lunch with the children who had been part of the original worm studies. We sat up at the front of the classroom, Jess silent but relaxed, as the students reminisced about the things we had done that year. When it was over, I asked Jess what she had noticed about our conversation: "They care about me," she wrote.

CONCLUSION

What did I learn from this child? Teaching is, to me, in many ways, the process of getting beyond whatever categories and preconceived notions we may have in order to see the individual child in real interaction with the world. The practice of close observation almost always leads to the revision of familiar ideas as well as sometimes official diagnoses. We see the individual in more and more detail. And we gain both a more open and a more complex idea of what thinking can look like and what people can be.

In a long career, I had had many experiences that suggested to me how interested children generally look, and how being concerned or interested or taking initiative might appear. And yet from watching Jessica closely and writing my notes, I came to see a greater variety in how students do these things. Although it is not certain that I was always correct in my understandings, working to include Jessica's point of view led me to treat her with more and more respect, and brought me closer to Michael Armstrong's (1990) challenge, to see "thought in all its forms."

My biggest insight, however, has to do with how observation and searching interpretation is felt by both sides. I can't prove it, but I believe she felt our relationship grow as much as I did. Her enormous gains were a part of this process, and in my case, as in many others in my experience, this process brought me much closer to someone unlike me, which is a gift in endless ways.

> **Each child, and each of us, highly particular, confers value on the world . . . . Each lends to the world a novel dimension, a particularized noticing that in the experience of it through the eyes of each of us has an enlarging effect on all.**
>
> —Patricia Carini, 2009

CHAPTER 9

Final Thoughts

I learned a great deal by stopping time and reflecting on what my students said and did. My relationships with my students were enhanced by this kind of attention and our joint learning was strengthened by the opportunity to think beyond the moment. I hope my readers can see this. But you may still wonder, will you have in your classes a Darius, a Jessica, a Cesar, will you teach children from many different countries, from different backgrounds, with such an array of unexpected (by me) ideas? Is what I learned from close observation and reflection on my particular students relevant to you, to teaching your students?

I share these stories here because I think this is the way others can gain from my experiences. I learned from stories written by the writers I have mentioned in Chapter 1. I felt that I experienced the children and the talk in these stories and the close attention paid. When I share my stories with colleagues and friends, I find that they often seem to enter the experience with me as well. When I write my stories, I learn from them again.

Exploring stories, alone or with others, keeps us aware of the complexity of other people, ourselves and our students. It keeps us asking what it means to learn and where learning can take us. And all of this leads us away from simply accepting our immediate view of a child or an event. Our assumptions, our evaluations, about others and about their ideas are made more visible to us and then they can be challenged.

Stories don't tell anyone what to do, or how to teach; rather they allow you to learn from empathy, from experience, from close attention over time.

I want to stress again though that these stories are not casual anecdotes. My commitment as a teacher in an inquiry tradition is to what I call ethnographic stories, that is, stories that especially value detail, even when these details seem at first irrelevant. My goal is to develop stories that arise first from close observation. I try, in my notes, to get down the words that were said as well as how they were said. Although they are often just scribbles at first, they are refined as I go back and remember more. I hope to keep these observations separate from my otherwise almost automatic interpretations and evaluations. I try always to assume, like ethnographers in the tradition of anthropology, that there is value in what seems at first unfamiliar and even unimportant and that I must look for that value. And I find that the more details I can include in my notes and stories, the more new understandings I am able to draw from each encounter.

Susan Sontag, the renowned thinker and critic, claimed that "any situation between people, when they are really human with each other, produces 'intelligence'" (Sontag, 2012). I believe there was something especially real or human in the moments I have described in this book. And in these moments, I think that the students were creating "intelligence." These were moments of joy for me—not necessarily right then, although often, but certainly in writing my notes, in recollection, in reading them, as I felt my students' thinking and their willingness to share it with me. The joy of teaching is one way to term this strong feeling of human connection based on joint experiences of thinking and discovering. The process of describing, of observing with care, of asking yourself why this child did something, what this child might mean or be thinking about—doing this creates a connection, a caring that deepens the relationship and creates joy.

Teaching as inquiry is teaching with the belief that every student has ideas and that these ideas are always relevant to important academic themes, and to personal ones as well. Teaching as inquiry is listening, and using notes and other documentation whenever possible, to stop time in order to listen better, to see anew. And it benefits enormously from reading widely, and from colleagues and mentors and friends who can help you gain distance from your own human assumptions, assumptions that stand in the way of seeing your students in their full individuality and humanity.

Teaching is a profession one grows in. We do not start out knowing how to teach. It is a human profession and, if things go well, we learn as we continue in it. However, we do not grow in our profession when we are simply told what to do, when we have little autonomy and little time for collegiality. I was fortunate in my school, my colleagues, and in the time in which I began teaching. I began teaching in the aftermath of the 1960s. It was a time of belief in children, and experimentation in teaching. We shared ideas and ideals. We had considerable autonomy. We believed we were making a new world and so we talked all the time to each other. Our principals were in many cases colleagues, supporting our inquiries. Still, it took learning a method to see beyond first assumptions into our students' strengths. It took time, too, and we had more of that than is available now. There is now less room in teaching for thinking, reflection, and choice. There is less room for collaboration. We are asked to do many tasks in addition to teaching. Teaching itself, what you do and when, is more and more controlled by others. Curricula are mandated; the time allotted to one area of study or another is determined by the administration; objectives and goals and, often, how to address them may not be the choice of the teacher.

It is hard to find the joy in a culture of teaching when others are telling you what to do, in a culture where you are always busy with little time for reflective choices of your own, where your meetings are consumed with directions and not with thinking about children.

When I read my notes, when I tell stories based on them and on what happened in the classroom, I feel joy and connection as I have said. And in addition, I feel an increased sense of agency—I hope the stories in this book both motivate and ground you as they have done for me. I hope they help you to take on the kind of listening and writing that enlivens the imagination and that leads to generous, humane interpretation. I hope they remind you that teaching must include feelings of joy and connection and that we must fight for that. I end with this sentence I have always loved from George Dennison's book *The Lives of Children* (1969/1990). George Dennison was a teacher. He did many other things in his life, wrote novels and plays, but for quite a few years he was a teacher. I can tell because he knew this:

> **Children are so powerfully attracted to the world that the very motion of their curiosity comes through to us as a form of love.**
>
> —Dennison, 1990

References

Armstrong, M. (1990). Another way of looking. *FORUM, 33*(1), 12–16.

Ball, D. (2018). Just dreams and imperatives: The power of teaching in the struggle for public education [Presidential address]. American Educational Research Association Annual Conference, New York, NY. https://www.youtube.com/watch?v=JGzQ7O_SIYY

Bang, M., Warren, B., Rosebery, A. S., & Medin, D. (2012). Desettling expectations in science education. *Human Development*, *55*, 302–318.

Barnes, D. (1992). *From communication to curriculum.* Boynton-Cook/Heinemann Publishers.

Beck, I., McKeown, M., & Kucan, L. (2002). *Bringing words to life: Robust vocabulary instruction.* Guilford Press.

Bertrand, M., & Marsh, J. (2015). Teachers' sensemaking of data and implications for equity. *American Educational Research Journal*, *52*(5), 861–893.

Brookline Teacher Researcher Seminar. (2004). *Regarding children's words: Papers from the Brookline Teacher Researcher Seminar.* Teachers College Press.

Carini, P. (2009). *Jenny's story: Taking the long view of the child: Prospect's philosophy in action.* Teachers College Press.

Cazden, C. (2001). *Classroom discourse: The language of teaching and learning* (2nd ed.). Heinemann.

Cazden, C. B., John, V. P., & Hymes, D. (Eds.). (1972). *Functions of language in the classroom.* Teachers College Press.

Cochran-Smith, M., & Lytle, S. (1993). *Inside outside: Teacher research and knowledge.* Teachers College Press.

Delpit, L. D. (1988). The silenced dialogue: Power and pedagogy in educating other people's children. *Harvard Educational Review*, *58*(3), 280–298.

Delpit, L. D. (2012). *"Multiplication is for white people": Raising expectations for other people's children.* New Press.

Dennison, G. (1999). *The lives of children: The story of the First Street School.* Heinemann. (Originally published 1969.)

DiCamillo, K. (2000). *Because of Winn-Dixie.* Candlewick Press.

Dutro, E. (2010). What "hard times" means: Mandated curricula, class-privileged assumptions, and the lives of poor children. *Research in the Teaching of English, 44*(3), 255–292.

Dyson, A. H. (1992). The case of the singing scientist: A performance perspective on the "stages" of school literacy. *Written Communication*, *9*(1), 3–47.

Enciso, P. (2003). Reading discrimination. In S. Green & D. Abt-Perkins (Eds.), *Making race visible: Literacy research for cultural understanding* (pp. 149–177). Teachers College Press.

Evans, M., Teasdale, R., Gannon-Slater, N., La Londe, P., Crenshaw, H., Greene, J. C., & Schwandt, T. (2019). How did that happen? Teachers' explanations for low test scores. *Teachers College Record*, 121(2), 1–40.

Flake, S. G. (2007). *Money hungry*. Hyperion.

Flake, S. G. (2018). *The skin I'm in*. Little, Brown.

Freire, P. (1993). *Pedagogy of the oppressed*. Continuum International Publishing Group.

Furman, C. E., & Traugh, C. E. (2021). *Descriptive inquiry in teacher practice*. Teachers College Press.

Gee, J. P. (2015). *Literacy and education*. Routledge.

Geertz, C. (1984). *Local knowledge: More essays in interpretive anthropology*. Basic Books.

González, N., Moll, L. C., & Amanti, C. (Eds.). (2006). *Funds of knowledge: Theorizing practices in households, communities, and classrooms*. Routledge.

Greene, M. (1978). *Landscapes of learning*. Teachers College Press.

Griffin, S. (2004). I need people. In Brookline Teacher Researcher Seminar, *Regarding children's words: Teacher research on language and literacy* (pp. 22–30). Teachers College Press.

Heath, S. B. (1983). *Way with words*. Cambridge University Press.

Himley, M., & Carini, P. (2000). *From another angle: Children's strengths and school standards*. Teachers College Press.

Himley, M. (2002). *Prospect's descriptive processes: The child, the art of teaching, the classroom and school*. Prospect Archives and Center for Education and Research. https://www.scribd.com/document/477146094/ProspectDescriptiveProcessesRevEd

Ladson-Billings, G. (2007). Pushing past the achievement gap: An essay on the language of deficit. *The Journal of Negro Education*, *76*(3), 316–323.

Lee, C. D. (1995). Signifying as a scaffold for literary interpretation. *Journal of Black Psychology*, *21*(4), 357–381.

Mayer, S. (2012). *Classroom discourse and democracy*. Peter Lang Publishing.

Michaels, S. (1981). "Sharing time": Children's narrative styles and differential access to literacy. *Language in Society*, *10*(3), 423–442.

Miletta, A. (2024). *Teach with confidence: Five domains for managing life in classrooms*. Rowman & Littlefield.

Myers, W. D. (2013). *Scorpions*. Amistad. (Original published 1988)

National Education Association. (2023). Trauma-informed practices. https://www.nea.org/professional-excellence/student-engagement/tools-tips/trauma-informed-practices

O'Connor, M. C., & Michaels, S. (1993). Aligning academic task and participation status through revoicing: Analysis of a classroom discourse strategy. *Anthropology and Education Quarterly*, *23*(4), 318–335.

Oláh, L., Lawrence, N., & Riggan, M. (2010). Learning to learn from benchmark assessment data: How teachers analyze results. *Peabody Journal of Education*, *85*(2), 226–245.

Paley, V. (1990). *The boy who would be a helicopter.* Harvard University Press.

Park, J., Simpson, L., Bickner, J., & Michaels, S. (2015). "When it rains a puddle is made": Fostering academic literacy in English learners through poetry and translation. *English Journal, 104*(4), 50–58. https://www.jstor.org/stable/24484322

Polacco, P. (1990). *Thunder cake.* Philomel.

Purcell-Gates, V. (1995). *Other people's words: The cycle of low literacy.* Harvard University Press.

Roosevelt, D. (1998). Teaching as an act of attention: An interview. *Changing Minds, 13*, 29–30.

Sachar, L. (1987). *There's a boy in the girls' bathroom.* Yearling.

Snow, C. (2002). *Reading for understanding: Toward an R&D program in reading comprehension.* RAND Corporation.

Sontag, S. (2012). A Sontag sampler. (2012, March 31). *The New York Times.* https://www.nytimes.com/2012/04/01/opinion/sunday/a-sontag-sampler.html

Spinelli, J. (1990). *Maniac Magee.* Little, Brown & Company.

Spinelli, J. (1997). *Crash.* Random House.

Spinelli, J. (2000). *Stargirl.* Scholastic.

Swaim, J. (2004). In search of an honest response. In Brookline Teacher Researcher Seminar, *Regarding children's words: Teacher research on language and literacy* (pp. 71–84). Teachers College Press.

Warren, B., & Rosebery, A. S. (1995). "This question is just too, too easy!": Perspectives from the classroom on accountability in science. National Center for Research on Cultural Diversity and Second Language Learning. https://eric.ed.gov/?id=ED390658

Index

About the Author

Cynthia Ballenger has been a public school teacher for many years. Her interest in listening to what children say was initially developed as a member of the Brookline Teacher Researcher Seminar. After teaching children regarded as having special needs, she later became a reading specialist and science teacher in K–8 schools. She has written numerous articles and two books on her teaching and her students.

She was educated at Barnard College and received her MSEd from Wheelock College. Her interest in language and culture led her to a PhD in Applied Linguistics from Boston University.

She taught at Brandeis University and Tufts University in their teacher preparation programs and has mentored a group of Teachers College graduates in teaching as inquiry. Her real love is teaching children. She continues to teach in her semi-retirement.

About the Author